About the Author

Rebecca is a busy working mum with a young son, she is married and has lived on the Fylde coast for over 40 years. She knows the difficulty of preparing a tasty meal on a budget. She inherited not only her great grandma's recipes, but also her grandma's – which include pre-World War 2 recipe books. She loves cooking and likes to adapt old and new recipes to keep the methods as simple and economical as possible.

Dedication

I would like to thank my son Danny and husband Gary who are my world – love you both so much. My mum Julie Newsham for all her support and her idea of posting cheap menu ideas on my Facebook page. My Stepdad Paul Newsham for many a word of wisdom. My Uncle Robert (Frowen) who has also spurred me on to make this dream a reality. My In laws Bill and Ann Inman – The Inman name lives on! My surrogate Grandma Ella – always gives me great advice. My good friends and colleagues who have provided me with their family recipes and also words of goodwill – in particular Sam– who created my logo, Heather who is like a personal motivational coach! Susan who was the one who prompted me to contact Austin Macauley. Jaime who has asked every day when a book is being published and also for supporting me throughout my 'Budget Menu Queen' journey .Also Tracy, Joanne and Karen – my great friends. I would like to thank all my Facebook likers as they have made my page the success it is. My BJFF family they have also supported me through my dreams to have my own recipe book. Penultimately I would like to thank my Grandma Margery Frowen – it was her recipes and ideas that have inspired me. Finally, Austin Macauley for 'taking a chance on me' and giving me an amazing opportunity.

Rebecca Inman

BUDGET MENU QUEEN

AUSTIN MACAULEY
PUBLISHERS LTD.

A CIP catalogue record for this title is available from the British Library.

ISBN 978 1 78455 181 0

www.austinmacauley.com

First Published (2015)
Austin Macauley Publishers Ltd.
25 Canada Square
Canary Wharf
London
E14 5LB

Printed and bound in Great Britain

Recipes

Slow Cooker Sausage and Mixed pepper savoury rice

Ingredients:
1 onion (1.5kg 79p FF) = 5p
400g pork sausages skinned and mashed with a fork (£1.55
specially selected Aldi 454g) = £1.36
150g Mixed peppers (66p 500g FF) = 19p
4 garlic cloves (39p 4 bulbs FF) = 4p
2 tsp smoked paprika (49p Aldi jar) = 2p
1 tsp coriander seeds (Rajah 100g Asda 76p) = 2p
250g long grain rice (59p 4 bags Aldi) = 30p
450ml chicken stock plus all-purpose seasoning = 3p
1 garlic baguette (34p Aldi) = 34p

Grand total = £2.35

Method:
Preheat the slow cooker, fry a little oil in a frying pan and add
the chopped onion cook for 3-4 minutes then add the sausage
meat, cooker until no longer pink. Add peppers and chopped
garlic cook for a further 3mins and then add the paprika and
coriander seeds and rice, then transfer to the slow cooker, then
cover all contents with enough stock to make sure all
ingredients are covered. Cook for 3 hours (if able stir half way
through) then serve with the garlic bread.

Spaghetti with Meatballs

Ingredients:
1 tsp oregano (49p Aldi jar) = 1p
1 potato diced (7.5kg £2.00 Farmfoods) = less than 1p
400g Fresh beef mince (750g Aldi £2.69) = £1.43
1 onion (79p 1.5kg FF) = 5p
1 egg (95p Aldi Free Range for 6) = 15p
400ml passata (500g 32p Aldi) = 25p
2 tbsp tomato puree (35p 200g Aldi) = 5p
450g Dried spaghetti (500g Aldi 23p) = 20p
4 tbsp flat leaf parsley (89p pot Aldi) = 22p
2 cloves garlic (39p 4 bulbs Farmfoods) = 2p
1 tsp plain four (45p 1.5kg Aldi) = 1p
5 tbsp veg oil (£1.19 Litre Aldi) = 5p

Grand Total = £2.45

Method:
Boil the diced potato for approx. 15 minutes until tender –
drain and mash. Combine the potato, beef, finely chopped
onion, egg, chopped garlic and parsley in a bowl – season to
taste. Spread out the flour on a plate and shape the meat into
walnut size pieces – roll in the flour and set to one side .Heat
the oil in a pan and add the meatballs to the oil, and cook on a
medium heat for approx. 10 minutes until golden all over. Add
the passata and puree and cook for a further 10 minutes until
the sauce is thickened.

Boil the spaghetti for approx. 10 minutes and serve with the
meatballs then
ENJOY!!

Hawaiian Pizza

Ingredients:
300g Strong white flour (1.5kg Aldi 75p) = 15p
1 tsp easy blend yeast (Lidl packet 25p –can be bought in all
supermarkets) = 1p
½ tsp salt = 1p
175ml hand hot water = free
1 tbsp olive oil = 2p
(Makes 4 7 ½ inch pizzas)
200g tomato puree (Aldi 35p 200g) = 35p...
50g Cheddar (1kg £5.00 FF) = 50p
3/4 packet finely chopped pancetta (99p Aldi) = 75p
100g pineapple (432g Tesco 50p) chopped into chunks = 11p
250g mozzarella (44p Aldi) = 44p
4 cloves garlic (39p 4 bulbs FF) = 4p
2 tsps oregano (49p jar Aldi) = 2p

Grand total for 4 pizzas = £2.40

Method:
Bases (My son loves making these). Sift the flour into a bowl
and add the yeast, oregano and salt, make a small well in the
top. Mix the water and oil and pour into the well, mix with a
round bladed knife and combine to make a sticky dough. Flour
a work surface and your hands then knead the dough for 10
minutes until smooth and elastic. Cover with cling film or a
clean damp towel for an hour until doubled in size. When risen
divide the dough into four and make into balls. Again roll out
on a floured surface turning a quarter after each roll. Preheat
the oven 220degrees and place the bases on baking trays (use
greaseproof paper) spread the puree over each base and
sprinkle with chopped garlic – spread to the edges. Sprinkle
the chopped pancetta and pineapple then top with chopped
mozzarella and grated cheddar. Bake for 10-12 minutes until
the cheese has melted – serve and ENJOY!

Mash potato/Ham and Pea Pie

Ingredients:
500g Potatoes (7.5kg £2.00 FF) = 10p
1 bay leaf = 1p
1 onion (79p 1.5kg FF) = 5p
100g frozen peas (1kg 99p Aldi) = 10p
30g Butter (98p 250g Aldi) = 11p
125ml Whole milk (£1.60 8 pints FF) = 5p
100ml Crème Fraiche (300ml 89p Aldi) = 29p
1 beaten egg (95p 6 Free Range Aldi) = 15p
80g Thick cooked ham (125g Aldi £1.79) = £1.14
90g Extra mature cheddar (350g £1.95 Aldi) = 50p

Grand Total = £2.50

Method:
Boil the potatoes with the bay leaf, Heat the oil in a pan and
add the onion, when the potatoes are boiled mash with the
butter/milk and crème fraiche. Season with S&P. Beat In the
egg and stir in the onions/peas/ham and ¾ cheese. Spread
evenly onto a casserole dish then sprinkle the rest of the cheese
on the top and bake at 190 degrees for 35-45 minutes until
bubbling and grill to brown.
Serve and ENJOY!!

Crispy baked fish with crushed new potatoes

Ingredients:
300g Basa Fillets (£1.99 Aldi 400g) = £1.50
1 onion (1.5kg 79p FF) = 5p
1 tomato (49p 6 FF) = 12p
2 slices of wholemeal bread made into crumbs (55p 800g Aldi)
= 5p
25g cheese (1 kg £5.00 extra mature FF) = 25p
1/2 tsp parsley (49p Aldi) – 1p
375g New potatoes (750g 85p Aldi) = 42p
100g Frozen peas (1kg 99p Aldi) = 10p

Grand Total = £2.50

Method:
Place the fish in an ovenproof dish and cover with thinly sliced
tomato and onion sprinkle the parsley on and season with S&P.
Grate the cheese and add to the breadcrumbs and sprinkle over
the fish.
Bake at 190 degrees for 30 minutes.
Boil the potatoes and when soft, drain and gently crush them
with the back of a fork and add a little butter, serve with the
fish and boiled peas.
Then Enjoy

Picnic Pie

Ingredients:
2 chicken breasts (£3.33 for 1kf FF) = 83p
½ packet Stuffing mix (37p Aldi Quixo) = 19p
2 sausages (£1.49 400g Aldi Pork & Leek) = 49p
1 beaten egg (95p Free Range for 6) = 15p
100g Leeks (66p 500g FF) = 13p
½ packet shortcrust pastry (375g 99p Aldi) = 50p
Serving Gravy (Quixo 79p for 23 servings) = 3p

Grand Total = £2.32

Method:
Season the chicken breasts, and cut into thin strips, Heat a little
oil in a pan and fry the chicken over a high heat then set aside.
Set aside 2 tbsp of the stuffing mixture and make up the rest
using half the amount of water the packet says.
Roll out 1/2 the pastry and put onto a pie tin (loose bottomed)
spoon the stuffing into the base and pack down well, arrange
the chicken over and squeeze the sausage meat from the skin
and press evenly over the top. Scatter over the rest of the dry
stuffing. Roll out the rest of the pastry and press down the
edges to seal, egg wash the pastry.
Bake at 180 degrees fan oven and 200 non fan for 50 minutes,
Brush after this time with the egg again and bake for another
10 minutes
Serve with the leeks and gravy…
ENJOY!!!

Crispy Chicken Bake

Ingredients:
1 onion (79p 1.5kg FF) = 5p
50g mixed peppers (500g 66p FF) = 6p
3 cooked chicken breasts (£3.33 FF 1 kg) = £1.24 (cut into
small pieces)
4 celery stalks (10 59p Aldi) = 23p
1 x 300g tin chicken soup (24p Asda Smart price) = 24p
100ml mayonnaise (500ml Aldi = 40p) = 8p
3 tbsp lemon juice (250ml Asda 39p) = 7p
50g Grated cheddar (1kg £5.00 FF) = 50p
1 bag ready salted crisps (12 Bags Asda 66p Smart Price) = 5p

Grand Total = £2.49

Method:
Preheat the oven to 180 degrees. Heat a little oil or water in a
frying pan and add the peppers, fry until soft. In a bowl mix
the chicken, celery, chicken soup, mayonnaise and lemon
juice. Put the mixture into a casserole/ovenproof dish. Open
the crisps and hold the opened end then crush with a rolling
pin/clean jar. Mix the crisps with the cheese and sprinkle on
the top. Bake for approx. 25mins until gold and bubbling.

Then ENJOY!

Piperade

Ingredients:
1 onion (79p 1.5KG Farmfoods) = 5p
150g Peppers (500G 66p FF) = 19p
2 cloves garlic (39p 4 bulbs FF) = 2p
3 peeled tomatoes (49p for 6 FF) = 25p
4 Eggs (95 p Free range Aldi) = 63p
400g Gammon steaks (1kg £3.33 FF) = £1.32

Grand Total = £2.46

Method:
Cook the gammon as per instructions. Heat a little oil in a pan
and cook the chopped onion until soft, Add peppers and finely
chopped garlic then cook for approx. 5 minutes, add roughly
chopped tomatoes and season with S&P. Cover and cook for
approx. 20mins. Lightly beat the eggs and then cover the
cooked veg and stir until about set. At the end of the gammon
cooking time – thinly slice it and divide – when the eggs are
set arrange the gammon on the top and serve immediately.

Then ENJOY!!!

Sweet and sour pork with stir fry veg noodles

Ingredients:

227g Pineapple chunks + 2 tsbps juice (540g 80p Tesco) = 15p
1 tbsp soy sauce (49p Home Bargains) = 1p
2 Tbsp Tomato Ketchup (Aldi 69p) = 2p
2 Tbsp white wine vinegar (59p Morrisons 250ml) = 2p
2 Tbsp Caster sugar (Aldi 1 kg 99p) = 1p
2 crushed garlic cloves (39p 4 bulbs Farmfoods) = 2p
2 tbsp cornflour (400g 65p Aldi) = 1p
400g Pork loin cut into thin strips (£3.33 1 kg Farmfoods) = £1.35
4 tbsp any oil – price depends on oil
1 red onion (49p 1 kg Aldi) = 7p
1 red pepper (89p Aldi 3 peppers) = 29p
2 sticks celery (49p Aldi approx. 8 stalks) = 12p
½ pack dried noodles (49p pack Aldi) = 25p
100g stir fry veg (66p 500g FF) = 13p

Grand Total = £2.45

Method:

Combine the pineapple juice, soy sauce, ketchup, vinegar, caster sugar and garlic in a jug then set aside. Boil the noodles until soft and set aside, heat a little oil in a pan just before the end of the pork cooking time and add the veg – fry until cooked through.
Place the cornflour and pork in a bowl and cover the pork in the flour. Heat half the oil in a wok/frying pan over a high heat, stir fry the pork until cooked through and set aside. Add the remaining oil to the pan and stir fry the onion, pepper and celery until tender. Return the pork to the pan with the pineapple chunks and the soy/ketchup mixture. Stir fry for about 1 minute until piping hot.
Serve with the noodles. ENJOY!!

Sausage Pie & Irish Champ

Ingredients:
200g Shortcrust pastry (375g 99p Aldi) = 52p
200g sausage meat (removed from skin) (454g £1.55 Aldi specially selected) = 68p
1 onion (79p 1.5kg FF) = 5p
4 rashers bacon (54 rashers £6.00 FF) = 5p
1 egg = (95p 6 free range Aldi) = 15p
15g lard or equivalent (250g 39p Aldi) = 2p
1tsp herbs (parsley/thyme any you have) = 1p
600g potatoes (7.5kg £2.00 FF) = 12p
Bunch of spring onions (50p Asda) = 50p
50g butter (250g 98p Aldi) = 19p
125ml milk (£1.60 8pints FF) = 5p
100g sweetcorn (66p 500g FF) = 13p

Grand Total = £2.47

Method:
Fry the chopped onion and bacon, then melt the lard or equivalent. Whisk the egg in a bowl add the sausage meat, onion, bacon , herbs and season with S&P.
Roll out 1/2 the pastry and line a pie tin or dish, spread the meat mix over the pastry and then add the other 1/2 rolled out pastry over the top. Brush with a little milk crimp the edges with the back or a fork or your fingers. Bake at 200 degrees for 15 minutes then 180 degrees for approximately 20-25 minutes. Meanwhile boil the potatoes for approximately 20mins (add a sprinkle of All purpose seasoning) Drain and return to a low heat. Place a clean towel over the top to allow them to dry out a little.
Heat the milk and finely chopped spring onions in a saucepan until warm. Mash the potatoes and butter until smooth and stir in the milk and spring onions, season and then serve with the pie and boiled sweetcorn.
Then ENJOY!!

Chicken & Chorizo Jambalaya

Ingredients:
2 Chicken breasts (£3.33 for 8 FF) = 83p
1 onion (1.5kg 79 p FF) = 5p
50g frozen peppers (500g 66p FF) = 6p
2 garlic cloves (39p 4 bulbs FF) = 2p
75g Chorizo sausage (99p 100g Tesco) = 74p
250g Long grain rice (1KG Aldi 40p) = 10p
1 tin plum tomatoes (Aldi 34p) = 34p
350ml chicken stock with all-purpose seasoning = 3p
1 tbsp Cajun seasoning (97p 108g Asda) = 5p

Grand Total = £2.22

Method:
Heat a little water in a pan and brown the chicken breasts (chopped into little pieces) until golden. Remove and set aside then put the onion in the pan cook until soft, add the pepper, garlic, chorizo and Cajun seasoning – cook for 5 minutes more.
Stir the chicken back in with the rice and add the tomatoes and stock. Cover and simmer for 20-25 minutes until the rice is tender – then ENJOY!!

Cheesy Bean and Sausage Bake

Ingredients

1 onion = 5p (FF 79p 1.5kg) = 5p
1 garlic clove (39p 4 bulbs) = 1p
1 x 400g tin of butter beans (39p Tesco East End) = 39p
(Or you could use baked beans)
1 x 400g tin chopped tomatoes (3 for £1 FF) = 34p
1 tbsp tomato puree (35p Aldi concentrate) = 5p
4 sausages (£1.55 specially selected Aldi) = 77p
50g extra mature cheddar (1kg £5.00 FF) = 50p
4 medium size potatoes to make jacket potatoes (7.5kg FF) =
10p
100g frozen leeks (66p 500g FF) = 13p

Grand Total = £2.34

Method:

Preheat the oven to 200 degrees.
Wrap the potatoes in foil and add to the oven (will need around
1 hour to 1 1/2 hours.
Fry the garlic and chopped onion in a little water (add some
all-purpose seasoning) . When soft stir in the beans, tomatoes,
tomato puree and sausages. Put the mixture into an ovenproof
dish – top with the grated cheese and cook for 30 minutes.
Serve with the jacket potatoes and boiled leeks.
Enjoy!!

Bacon & Egg Muffins

Ingredients:
4 slices of bread (55p 800g Aldi) = 11p
8 Eggs (95p 6 free range Aldi) = £1.28
5 slices bacon halved (£6.00 54 rashers FF) = 55p
20g Grated Cheese (1 kg £5.00 extra mature FF) = 20p
1 tin baked beans (3 for £1.00 FF) = 34p

Grand Total = £2.48

Method:
Preheat oven to 200 degrees.
In a frying pan cook the bacon allowing it to be flexible not raw, using a circular cookie cooker, scone cutter or a clean jam jar – cut 2 circles out of each slice of bread.
Lightly grease a muffin tin, lay a circle of bread in each muffin section and wrap the bacon around the inside of each muffin section. Sprinkle a little cheese on each bread circle. Carefully crack an egg into each 'muffin' then add the tray to the oven and cook until the eggs are set to your liking (approximately 15mins) dependent on how runny you want the yolks. When the eggs are set – remove each from the pan and serve with heated beans.

Enjoy!!

Stuffed Peppers

Ingredients:
4 peppers (89p for 3 Aldi) = £1.20
225g Minced beef and onion (800g £2.50 FF) = 70p
1 onion finely chopped (1.5kg 79p) = 5p
50g Mushrooms (66p for 500G) = 6p
2 tomatoes (6 for 49p FF) = 16p
1 slice of bread – toasted and cubed (55p 800g Aldi) = 5p
1/4 tsp Worcester sauce (150g Tiger Tiger £1.00 Asda) = 1p
1 bag boil in the bag rice cooked (59p 4 bags Aldi) = 15p

Grand Total for 4 = £2.38

Method:
Wash and dry the peppers, cut off the tops and remove the
seeds and membrane. Pre-cook in boiling water for 5 minutes
and drain. Season with s&p. In a non-stick pan fry the beef and
chopped onion, stir in the mushrooms and finely chopped
tomatoes, bread, rice and Worcester sauce. Season to taste
once again and spoon the mixture into each pepper then bake
in a preheated oven 180 degrees for approximately 25 minutes
(sprinkle with a little cheese if required) serve and
ENJOY!

Chicken Fajitas

Ingredients:
200g Defrosted chicken breasts cut into small pieces (£3.33
1kg FF) = 66p
100g mixed frozen peppers (66p 500g FF) = 13p
1/4 bottle BBQ sauce (Asda on offer Heinz sticky BBQ sauce
500g £1.00) = 25p
1 onion (1.5kg 79p FF) = 5p
1 clove garlic (39p 4 bulbs FF) = 1p
8 Tortilla wraps (Aldi 85p) = 85p
100g grated cheese (Aldi 350g Cheese Emporium Mature
cheddar – £1.95) = 55p

Grand Total = £2.50

Method:
Marinate the Chicken/sliced onion/peppers for approximately
1/2 hour. Heat oil in a pan and then add the finely chopped
garlic. Heat the wraps as per instructions in the oven. Add the
chicken mixture to the hot pan and fry until cooked. Place the
cheese and chicken mixture into individual bowls and
everyone can make their own wraps-can get messy!
Remove the wraps – place a little chicken mixture and grated
cheese in the middle and fold up the bottom half of the wrap
and wrap over each side of the bottom flap and ENJOY!

Fully Loaded Potato Skins

Ingredients:

500g Large potatoes £2.00 7.5kg FF) = 10p
110g Mature cheddar (350g £1.95 Aldi) = 62p
125ml Sour Cream (89p Aldi 300ml) = 37p
1/2 bunch spring onions (50p Asda bunch) = 25p
1/2 tsp salt (store cupboard)
6 rashers pancetta (packet of approximately 12 99p Aldi) = 50p
1/2 packet pre made salad (49p Aldi Everyday essentials) = 25p
75g Fresh cherry tomatoes (75p 300g Aldi) = 18p
20g Salad crispies (Asda 100g £1.18) = 23p

Grand Total = £2.50

Method:

Prepare the salad set to one side.
Preheat your oven to 200C/180C fan/400F/gas 6 and bake the potatoes (pricking them first) for about 1½ hours, or until the skins are crisp and the insides fluffy. When they cool, cut them in half lengthways and scoop the insides into a bowl.
Put the husk-like skins of the potatoes on a tray and, when cool, cover until you are ready to fill them. Let the potato cool in the bowl, and then cover until needed.
Grate the cheese, and add 200g of it to the cold potato along with the sour cream. Chop the spring onions and add to the potato, with the salt. Spoon the potato filling into the potato skins, and lay each half on a baking tray so they fit snugly together. Sprinkle over the remaining cheese, giving each potato skin a light covering, and cook for 20-30 minutes until golden.
Fry (or grill) the bacon rashers in oil until crispy, then crumble them and sprinkle over each potato skin to make them fully loaded.
Serve with the salad and ENJOY!!

Coconut Dahl & Roasted Sweet potato

Ingredients:
1 Sweet potato (on offer at Aldi 69p for 4) = 17p
1 tsp cumin seeds (Asda Rajah 100g 78p) = 1p
200g Red Lentils (Tesco whole foods 1kg £1.79) = 35p
1 400ml tin coconut milk (Aldi 79p – although Home Bargains and B&Ms have it cheaper) = 79p
1 onion (FF 1.5kg 79p) = 5p
4 cloves of garlic (39p 4 Bulbs FF) = 4p
1 tsp medium curry powder (TRS Asda 100g 49p) = 1p
1 tsp turmeric (Asda TRS 100g 62p) = 1p
Torn fresh coriander (49p living pot Aldi) = 5p
4 Naan bread (49p for 2 Aldi) = 98p

Grand total for 4 = £2.46

Method:
Preheat the oven 200 degrees (180 fan) and put the peeled and sliced sweet potato on a baking tray – sprinkle with cumin seeds and a little oil then roast for approximately 20 minutes or until soft.
Put the lentils in a pan and add the turmeric and coconut milk. Pour over 250ml water and bring to the boil. Simmer for 15 minutes or until the lentils are soft (add more water if needed) Heat a little oil in a frying pan and add the chopped onion and garlic and fry until soft Stir in the curry powder then add to the coconut mixture. Divide into 4 serving bowls – top with the roasted sweet potato, sprinkle on the chopped coriander and serve with the warmed Naan breads – then ENJOY!!

Creamy Salmon Tagliatelle

Ingredients:
250g salmon fillets (£3.33 500g FF) = £1.66
1 veg stock cube with a little all- purpose seasoning with a
little water (3p)
1 onion (1.5kg 79p FF) = 5p
200g tagliatelle (£1.00 500g Asda) = 40p
100g frozen peas (1kg 99p Aldi) = 10p
75ml crème fraiche (300ml 89p Aldi) = 22p

Grand Total for 4 = £2.46

Method:
Preheat the oven 220 degrees and bake the salmon for
approximately 15mins (add a dab of butter on the fillets)
Bring 1 1/4 pints of water to the boil, add the stock and
chopped onion then add the tagliatelle – cook for 5 minutes.
Add the frozen peas to the pasta pan and cook for a further 5
minutes until tender. Drain the pasta and leave a little of the
seasoned water in the pan. Return the drained pasta to the pan
and stir in the crème fraiche. Remove the cooked salmon from
the oven and remove any skin. Then flake into small pieces
and add to the pasta and crème fraiche mixture – stir all the
ingredients through together and season well with salt and
ground black pepper.
Serve and ENJOY!!

Chicken Kiev

Ingredients:

4 tbsp softened butter (98p 250g Asda's own) = 15p
4 garlic cloves (39p 4 bulbs FF) = 4p
1 tbsp fresh parsley (49p bundle Aldi) = 5p
1 tbsp dried oregano (49p Aldi) = 2p
4 chicken breasts – approx 100g each (£3.33 1.5kg FF) = £1.33
85g fresh white breadcrumbs (800g loaf Aldi) = 6p
1 beaten egg (95p 6 Free Range Aldi) = 15p
1/4 bottle parmesan (59p B&Ms) = 15p
150ml veg oil for deep frying (£1.09 Aldi 1 litre) = 16p
2 bags boil in the bag rice (59p Aldi) = 30p

Grand Total for 4 = £2.41

Method:

Place the garlic (finely chopped) in a bowl with the butter and mix well. Stir in the herbs and season with salt and pepper. Pound the chicken breasts (defrosted) with a rolling pin to flatten to even thickness – then place a tablespoon of the butter mix into the centre of each one. Secure with cocktail sticks.

Combine the breadcrumbs and parmesan on a plate. Dip the chicken parcels in the beaten egg and coat in the breadcrumb mixture. Then chill in the fridge for 30 minutes. Remove after 30 minutes and coat in the egg again and then the breadcrumb mixture.

Pour the oil in a deep sided frying pan, and heat until a cube of bread fried in 30 seconds – then transfer the chicken to the oil and fry for approximately 5 minutes (turn when browned on one side) . Lift out the chicken and drain on kitchen paper.

Serve with the cooked boiled rice and ENJOY!!!

(Tip when you have mixed the butter/garlic and herbs – leave to harden in the fridge until solid again – so it won't melt too quickly when frying) .

Greek Stifado (Slow Cooker) with crusty bread rolls

Ingredients:
225g Beef steak (450g £2.50 FF) = £1.25
150g Minced beef (800g £2.50 FF) = 46p
2 tbsp red wine vinegar (80p Tesco 350ml) = 2p
1 tsp cinnamon = 1p
1/2 tsp grated nutmeg (95p Tesco) = 1p
2 garlic cloves (39p 4 cloves FF) = 2p
3 fresh tomatoes (49p for 6 FF) = 24p
1 tsp ground cloves (35g 95p Asda/Tesco/Morrisons) = 1p
1 tbsp tomato puree (35p Aldi tube concentrate) = 2p
450ml stock plus spoon of All purpose seasoning = 3p
1 tsp thyme (49p Aldi) = 1p
75g Shallots (£1.00 Asda 450g) = 16p
Packet of crusty bread mix (Aldi 500g 65p makes 10 bread rolls)
MAKE 4 OF THESE = 20p
GRAND TOTAL FOR 4 = £2.44

Method:
Preheat the slow cooker, Put a little oil in a pan (or fry with water) add the meat – season and fry for about 6 minutes.
Increase the heat and then add the red wine vinegar. Cook for a few minutes then add the cinnamon, nutmeg, garlic and ground cloves and cook for a further minute.
Add the roughly chopped tomatoes and puree – then the stock and cook for a few minutes then transfer to the slow cooker.
Pour in the stock and add the thyme – cover and cook on a low heat for approximately 8 hours. About an hour before the end of the cooking time, heat some more oil in a pan and fry the shallots and then when softened and browned add to the slow cooker.

Bake the rolls as per instructions on the packet ready to dip in the Stifado when ready.
ENJOY!!

Teriyaki Chicken

Ingredients:
450g Chicken Breasts (£3.33 for a kilo FF) – £1.66
1/4 bottle of soy sauce (49p HB bottle) = 12p
2 tbsps Brown Sugar (79p for 500G Aldi) = 2p
1/2 teaspoon lazy ginger (49p jar HB) = 1p
2 tbsp white wine vinegar (80p 350 ml Asda) = 3p
1 clove garlic (39p 4 bulbs FF) = 1p
2 tbsp tomato ketchup (69p Aldi 563g) = 2p
1/2 packet dried noodles (49p full packet Aldi) = 25p
100g Stir fry veg (66p for 500g FF) = 12p

Grand total for 4 = £2.25

Method:
Mix all the ingredients together (apart from the chicken/noodles and veg) to make a marinade. Add thinly sliced chicken slices or chunks and make sure all the chicken is covered and soaked in. Leave for approximately 30 minutes.

Boil the noodles and heat some oil in a frying pan or wok, when very hot add the chicken and fry lightly, add in the stir fry veg and the boiled drained noodles. Fry for a few more minutes until everything is mixed together and covered in the marinade – serve and ENJOY!!!!

Rissoles & Gravy

Ingredients:
500g Minced beef (£2.50 for 800g FF) = £1.56
1 onion (79p 1.5kg FF) = 5p
2 garlic cloves (39p for 4 bulbs FF) = 2p
2tbsp Tomato paste (35p Aldi) = 5p
2-3 tbsp Dijon mustard (185g 58p Asda) = 14p
1 tbsp dried parsley (49p jar Aldi) = 2p
1 tbsp dried chives (86p jar Asda) = 2p
2 eggs (95p for 6 Free range Aldi) = 30p
100g breadcrumbs (800g loaf Aldi 55p) = 6p
Splash of milk and flour for dusting.
500g potatoes to make mash (7.5kg £2.00 FF) = 10p
100g peas (1kg 99p Aldi) = 10p
1 serving gravy (75p 300g Aldi) = 7p

Grand Total for 4 = £2.49

Method:
Boil the potatoes to make a mash at the end of the Rissoles cooking time .combine the mince /chopped onions/ chopped garlic/tomato puree/mustard/herbs and 1 egg in a bowl. Season with salt and pepper. Shape into patties by pressing small handfuls into small balls and flattening. Lightly dust each one with flour. Whisk the other egg and add a little milk. Dip the patties one at a time and then in the breadcrumbs. Heat any oil in a pan and fry each side for 3-4 minutes. (May have to be in batches) .
Heat the peas and serve with the mash /gravy and rissoles.
ENJOY!

Mozzarella and basil stuffed chicken wrapped in bacon and served with garlic new potatoes

Ingredients:
500g Chicken breasts defrosted (£10.00 for 5kg Asda) = £1.00
1packet mozzarella (44P Aldi) = 44p
Fresh basil ¼ pot (89p living pot Aldi) = 22p
4 bacon rashers (£6.00 for 54 rashers FF) = 11p
1 garlic bulb = 1 p
New potatoes (£1.14 750g) = 57p
1 tbsp butter – price depends on which butter.
10g Grated extra mature cheddar (5kg £5.00 FF) = 10p

Grand total for 4 = £2.45

Method:
Defrost the chicken and split the breasts in half, Slice the mozzarella and place inside the breasts along with the basil leaves. Fold the top over the mozzarella and basil and then wrap a rasher of bacon around each breast. Wrap in foil and cook for approx. 40 mins 200 degrees remove the foil when cooked and sprinkle a little grated cheese over each chicken breast. Grill to brown.

Approximately 20 minutes before the end of the chicken breast cooking time – Boil the potatoes and when cooked drain and stir in melted butter with finely chopped garlic.

Serve together.

Crofters Roll with Latkes (potato pancakes)

Ingredients:
225g cooked minced beef (500g £2.50 FF) = £1.25
1 rasher of bacon (chopped) (54 rashers £6.00 FF) = 9p
1 small onion (1.5kg 79p FF) = 5p
1 tsp mixed herbs = 1p
Salt and pepper to season
100g Fresh breadcrumbs (800g loaf 55p Aldi) = 7p
Stock cube & AP seasoning 3p

For the Latkes:
450g potatoes (peeled and grated) (7.5kg FF £2.00) = 9p
1 onion (as above) 5p
Salt and pepper to season
1/2 tsp dried parsley = 1p
1 separated egg (95p for 6 free range Aldi) = 15p
1 tbsp flour (45p 1.5kg Aldi) = 1p

Grand Total for 4 = £1.81

Method:
For the Crofters Roll – Bind the cooked mince/chopped bacon rasher/onions/herbs/ salt & pepper and breadcrumbs gradually bind with the made up stock. Shape into a roll and bake on a baking sheet for 30 minutes at 180 degrees. Can be served hot or cold.
For the Latkes:
Drain and excess water from the grated potatoes and mix in the grated onion, Salt & pepper ,parsley and egg yolk. Mix in the flour whisk the egg white until stiff and fold in the potato mixture. Form into flat cakes and then shallow fry until golden and serve with the Roll.
Then Enjoy!!

Savoury Glazed Meatloaf with Bubble & Squeak

Ingredients:
500g Minced beef (800g £2.50 FF) = £1.56
70g breadcrumbs price depends on bread price – can use stale bread.
1 onion (79p 1.5kg FF) = 5p
1egg (95pfor 6 Aldi) = 15p
1 tbsp worcs sauce (tiger tiger Asda) = 1p
2 tbsp tomato sauce (Bramwells 69p Aldi) = 2p
185g Evaporated milk (410g NuMe Morrisons 57p) = 25p
15g mustard powder = 3p
1 tbsp brown sugar (Brown Sugar (Silver spoon 500g AL = 79p) = 2p
1/2tsp mustard powder extra = 2p
¼ cup of tomato ketchup extra = 7p
¼ Cabbage (49p full one) = 12p
1 onion (1.5kg 79p) = 5p
200g mash (7.5kg £2.00 FF) = 4p

Grand Total for 4 = £2.39

Method:
Combine beef / breadcrumbs/onion/egg/sauces /milk and mustard in a medium bowl. Press the mixture in a loaf tin approx. 180x160. Turn tin upside down into a foil lined tray. Leave the tin in place and cook for 15 minutes at 180 degrees. Combine Sugar /mustard and ketchup – after 15 minutes remove from the tin-brush the loaf with the glaze and then cook for a further hour or until well browned and cooked through.

Bubble and squeak: Slice and finely chop ¼ cabbage, finely chop the onion, add the mash and make into patties. Melt A little butter in a pan and add the patties coating each with butter, when browned flip and cook the other side. Then serve with the meatloaf.

Prawn Madras & Boiled Rice

Ingredients:
165g Frozen Prawns (£2.99 325g Aldi) = £1.62
2 onions (79p 1.5kg FF) = 10p
2 Garlic cloves (39p for 4 bulbs FF) = 2p
2 tsp ginger (59p 220g HB) = 2p
1 tsp each of Turmeric/curry powder/Ground Cumin and
Garam Masala (all Asda 100g between 68-72p) = 4p
½ tsp chopped chili (59p 220g jar HB) = 1p
1 tin chopped tomatoes (£1.00 for 3 FF) = 33p
2 bags boil in the bag rice (59p for 4 Aldi) = 30p

£2.44 Grand Total for 4.

Method:
Dry fry the onions and garlic in a non- stick pan until soft and
then add the spices. Add the chili and tomatoes .Add 100ml
water and simmer for 10 minutes. Season the sauce with S &
P. Add the prawns and cook for a further 2 minutes then serve
with the cooked boiled rice.

Then ENJOY!!

Kedgeree

Ingredients:
250g Smoked Haddock (500g £2.79 Aldi) = £1.39
2 bay leaves = 2p
300ml milk = 15p (8 pints for £1.60 FF) = 13p
4 eggs (Aldi Free Range 95p for 6) = 64p
1 tsp parsley = 1p
1 tsp coriander = 1p
1 chopped onion (79p 1.5 KG) = 5p
1 tsp ground coriander = 1p
1 tsp turmeric = 1p
2 tsp curry powder = 1p
1 bag of boil in the bag rice (59p for 4 Aldi) = 12p
50g frozen peas. (1kg 99p Aldi) = 6p

Grand Total for 4 = £2.46

Method:
Boil the Rice and whilst cooking – poach the haddock in milk
/bay leaves/parsley and coriander & cook through. Hard boil
the eggs and then heat some oil in a pan. Add the onion
/ground coriander /turmeric and curry powder, keep stirring
and when the rice is boiled (you can pre- cook this to ensure all
ready at the same time) remove from the bag, drain the fish
from the milk mixture and flake into pieces. Add the fish / rice
and peas to the onion mixture and coat everything. When all is
blended together
- shell the hard boiled eggs and cut into quarters. Put the
kedgeree in bowls/plates and top with the quartered eggs.
Then
ENJOY!!

Beef & Leek Cous Cous

Ingredients:
150g Leeks (66p for 500g FF) = 20p
500g Minced Beef (£2.50 for 800g FF) = £1.56
2 Fresh Chillies (49p for pack Aldi) = 25p
2 tsp Paprika (49p 50g – Aldi) = 2p
6 Garlic Cloves (39p for 4 bulbs FF) = 6p
450ml Beef stock plus tsp All Purpose Seasoning = 3p
225g Cous Cous (68p Asda 500g) = 34p
2 tsp dried Parsley = 2p

Grand Total for 4 £2.48

Method:
Preheat the oven to 150g heat a little (any) oil in a frying pan and add the leeks – cook until soft, Add the mince then brown.

Stir in chillies, paprika, parsley, chopped garlic and cook for 5 minutes, add the stock and combine – then stir in the Cous Cous. Transfer to a casserole dish and cook for 15 minutes – stir then serve
ENJOY!!

Sausage Plait with Mash & Peas

Ingredients:
340g Frozen puff pastry – defrosted (66p FF) = 66p
200g Sausages – removed from the skin (454g Butchers
selection £1.49 Aldi) = 55p
1 onion (1.5kg FF) = 5p
1/2 tin chopped tomatoes drained (34p tin Aldi) = 17p
50g defrosted mushrooms (66p 500g FF) = 6p
1 tsp mixed herbs = 1p
500g potatoes (7.5 kg FF £2.00) = 10p
100g Frozen pea...s (99p 1kg Aldi) = 10p
1 serving Gravy granules (75p 300g Quixo meat gravy) = 7p

Grand Total for 4 = £1.77

Method:
Prepare the potatoes and boil for the mash – season with a little
all-purpose seasoning.
Mix the sausage meat/mushrooms /chopped onions/ sieved
tomatoes and herbs. Roll out the pastry – place the meat
mixture in the middle of the pastry and then cut thick diagonal
strips down the sides of the pastry. Then plait it. Brush with a
little milk. Bake in a preheated oven 180degrees for 20
minutes then reduce the heat to 150 and bake for a further 20
minutes.
Make up the mash just before the end of the baking time – add
a little butter and milk.
Heat the peas and make up the gravy.
Cut up the plait and serve with the mash/peas and gravy – then
...
ENJOY!!

Pork Apple and Potato Bake

Ingredients:
400g thinly sliced potatoes (7.5kg FF = £2.00) = 8p
4 Pork loin steaks (£3.33 for 10 FF) = £1.33
2 Onions chopped (79p 1.5kg FF) = 10p
3 Apples de-cored, wedged and sliced (89p for 7 Aldi) = 38p
3 Tomatoes wedged or sliced (79p for 6 Aldi but 49p for 6 FF)
= 34p (based on Aldi tomatoes)
500ml any stock and All- purpose seasoning = 3p
1 tsp sage = 1p
175g Roasting veg (66p for 500g FF) = 20p

GRAND Total for 4 = £2.47

Method:
Preheat the Oven to 200degrees (180 for fan and Gas6) Add a
little oil to a casserole dish and add the thinly slices
potatoes/sage and season. Cook for 15 minutes.

Heat a little oil in a frying pan and brown the pork on both
sides, remove from the pan and then fry the onions for 5
minutes.
Remove the potatoes from the oven, and turn down by 20
degrees and 2 on gas. Arrange the pork/onions/apples and
tomatoes over the potatoes, pour over the stock and bake for
30minutes or until the pork is tender. Also cook the roasting
veg as per instructions (you may want to cook before the apple
bake as they need cooking at a higher temperature then keep
them warm until the bake is ready)

ENJOY!!

Lamb & Bacon Burgers

Ingredients
250g minced lamb (FF 500g = £2.50) = £1.25
50g fresh wholemeal breadcrumbs (45p E.Essentials Aldi) =
3p
1 small onion, chopped finely (FF 79p 1.5kg) = 5p
2 tsps dried oregano = 2p
2 smoked back bacon rashers, de-rinded and chopped finely
(99p for 6 rashers FF)
= 33p
1/2 medium size egg, beaten (Aldi 99p for 6) = 7p
Salt and freshly ground black pepper
4 rolls split (55p for 6 Aldi) = 36p
Shredded 1/4 iceberg lettuce (48p Aldi full lettuce) = 12p
2 thinly sliced tomatoes (49p for 6 FF) = 17p

Grand total for 4 = £2.40

Method:
In a large bowl, mix together the lamb, breadcrumbs, onion,
oregano, bacon and seasoning. Bind together with the egg. (I
also added a little grated cheese) Divide the mixture into 6, roll
into balls and flatten with the palm of your hand. Chill in the
refrigerator for 30 minutes.

Place the burgers under a preheated grill/broiler and cook for 5
– 6 minutes each side, or until cooked through. Serve each
burger in a warm toasted roll filled with a lettuce and tomato
garnish.

ENJOY!!

Bacon and potatoes

Ingredients:
1 kg potatoes (7.5kg £2.00 Farmfoods) 20p
I packet defrosted bacon cut into smaller strips (£1.00
Farmfoods) = £1.00
2 Onions (79p bag Aldi) = 20p
1 serving onion gravy (75p 23 servings Aldi Quixo) = approx.
5p
Grated cheese 100g (1kg £5.00 Farmfoods) = 50p

Grand Total for 4 = £1.95

Method:
Slice the potatoes quite thinly lengthways (after peeling) and
slice the onion thinly – then boil until just about soft. Lightly
fry the bacon and then layer between the potatoes /onion.

Top with a layer of potatoes and make up a serving of gravy
but add more water than instructed – want the gravy quite
runny. Then pour over the potatoes and top with grated cheese
and grill – I love this!!! You can use sausages instead of the
bacon or turkey rashers (but a lot more expensive)

ENJOY!!

Slow Cooker Pork & Potato Hot Pot

Ingredients:
2 Onions (79p 1.5kg Aldi) = 10p
1 Clove of Garlic (39p 4 bulbs FF) = 1p
225g Frozen Mushrooms (66p for 500g FF) = 33p
1/4tsp Sage = 1p
900g Peeled , Thinly sliced potatoes (£2 for 7.5kg FF) = 18p
1 1/4 pints veg or chicken stock with All Purpose seasoning) = 3p
4 Pork Chops (£3.33 for 8 FF) = £1.66
...
Grand Total = £2.32

(Optional: Pickled Red Cabbage 65p Sainsbury's 326g)

Method:
Grease the slow cooker pot with a little butter and preheat.
Heat any oil in a frying pan and add thinly sliced onions,
Garlic and Mushrooms. Fry for approx. 5 minutes and add the
herbs. Spoon half the mushroom mixture in the base of the
slow cooker pot and arrange half the potato slices on the top.
Season with S&P. Trim any fat off the chops and place on top
of the potatoes, pour over half the stock.
Repeat the Mushroom and potato layers and pour the stock
over the top of the final layer or potatoes. Dot a little butter on
the top of the potatoes – then slow cook on low for at least 5
hours. Grill to brown at the end if preferred and serve with a
little pickled cabbage (optional) then:

ENJOY!!!!

Arroz Con Pollo

Ingredients:
6 chicken thighs (half a bag of £3.33 Farmfoods frozen chicken thighs) = £1.66
1 onion (Aldi 79p) = 10p
1/2 tin chopped tomatoes (34p Aldi) 19p
50g frozen mixed pepper (66p 500g Farmfoods) = 13p
2 garlic cloves (Farmfoods 39p 4 bulbs) = 2p
1 tsp paprika (try and get smoked but not hot) = 1p
1 bay leaf (52p for a box from most supermarkets) = 1p
1 tsp thyme (49p 50g jar Aldi) = 2p
1 tsp oregano (49p 50g jar Aldi) = 2p
1 bag long grain rice (59p 4 bags Bilash rice Aldi) = 15p
750 ml chicken stock (10 stock cubes Tesco 20p) = 2 p
2 tsp tomato puree (Aldi double concentrated puree tube 35p) = 5p
10 ml lemon juice (85p for 500ml from Aldi) = 1.7p
Salt and pepper
100g frozen peas (99p 1kg bag Aldi) = 10p

Grand total for 4 = £2.50

Method:
Preheat the oven to 180 degrees 200 non assisted.
Heat some oil in a deep sided frying pan. Evenly brown the chicken, remove (when browned) and set aside. Reduce the heat and fry the chopped onion until soft /add peppers and garlic. Add the paprika/bay leaf /tomatoes/thyme and oregano and stir in the (dried – removed from the bag) rice. Fry for a couple of minutes stirring constantly. Add the stock /puree and lemon juice and season with salt and pepper.

Transfer everything to a casserole dish and cover with the chicken thighs (pushing down the rice) cook for 15 minutes then add the frozen peas. Cook for a further 10 minutes until the rice is soft or until all the liquid has been absorbed.
Serve immediately and ENJOY!!!!

Chicken sautéed Leek and Pancetta in a cheesy sauce with sage boiled potatoes

Ingredients:

500g (Farmfoods frozen chicken £3.33 for a kilo bag) = £1.66
Bisto cheese granules (£1.25 makes 23 servings) = 5p
1/4 packet of pancetta (99p Aldi) = 25p
100g frozen leeks (66p for 500g Farmfoods) = 13p
500g peeled washed potatoes (£2.00 for 7.5kg Farmfoods) = 13p
Stock cube (20p for 10 Tesco Value) = 5p
1/2 teaspoon sage 1p
(Optional mushrooms) 100g frozen (Farmfoods 66p for 500g) = 13p

Total cost for a family of 4 £2.27 without mushrooms or £2.40 with mushrooms

Method:

Put the chicken breasts in an ovenproof dish – crumble half the stock cube into approx. 250ml hot water and pour over the chicken. The chicken will then not dry out....follow instructions on the back of the packet re cooking time – will take approx. 45mins.Prepare the potatoes -peeling/washing and cutting into preferred chunks for boiled potatoes. Crumble over the remaining stock cube and add a 1/2 teaspoon of sage. Later add boiling water (will take approx. 20 minutes to cook) so will need to get on the hob approx. halfway through the chicken cooking time.

Sautee the leeks (and mushrooms if required) approximately 10 minutes before the end of the chicken cooking time. Add finely chopped pancetta and fry until the leeks are soft and the pancetta is cooked. (sauté in a bit of butter)

Make up the cheese sauce following the instructions and add to the leeks pancetta (mushroom mixture) and then after checking the chicken has cooked and has been divided to 4 portions transfer the chicken to plates – cover with the sauce and serve with the boiled potatoes.

ENJOY!!

Sausage Casserole

Ingredients:
500g potatoes (7.5kg Farmfoods £2.00) = 13p
50g carrots (1 kg bag Aldi 79p) = 20p
8 sausages (99P Aldi) = 99p
2 tbsp oil price depends on oil – but minimal cost.
1 chopped onion (79p for approx. 7 – 8 Aldi) 10p
1 garlic clove (crushes) (39p 4 bulds Farmfoods) 1p
1 tsp sage (49p 50g Aldi) 1p
400g can chopped tomatoes (Sweet Harvest 24p Aldi) = 24p
400ml stockpot stock (99p for 4 Home Bargains) = 25p
1-2 bay leaves (52p packet from most supermarkets) = 2p

Grand total for 4 = £1.95

Method:
Turn the oven to 180°C/fan160°C/gas 4. Peel the potatoes cut into quarters. Peel the carrots and cut into about 4 or 5 pieces. Prick the sausages all over with a fork – this helps the fat to run out of the sausages, so that they don't split open as they cook. Heat the olive oil in a heavy-based casserole dish and fry the sausages, moving them around until lightly golden / should take about 10 minutes. Remove from the pan and put aside.
Add the chopped onion to the casserole (there will still be some oil in the pan from the sausages) and continue to cook over a low heat for 5-10 minutes, until the onion is slightly soft. Add the garlic and sage and cook for another minute.
Add the chopped potatoes and carrots and stir everything around in the casserole so that the vegetables are coated with the oil.
Add the tomatoes and stockpot stock (to measure the stock, you can use the empty tomato can – filled up, it will hold 400ml of stock) and the bay leaves. Bring to a simmer (so it's just bubbling gently) . Return the sausages to the casserole. Put the casserole into the oven. Cook for 45 minutes, until the potatoes are cooked through, and serve. ENJOY!!

Chicken Gumbo – a rich Cajun stew

Ingredients:

500G Chicken thighs (1kg bag Farmfoods 3.33) = £1.66
1 onion (79p bag Aldi) = 10p
2 garlic cloves (39p 4 bulbs Farmfoods) = 2p
2 celery sticks (Aldi approx. 8 sticks 49p) = 10p
50g frozen mixed peppers (500g = 66p Farmfoods) = 6p
1 bay leaf (approx. 52p box from supermarkets) = 1p
2 tbsps Plain flour (49p 1.5kg Aldi) = 2p...
20g Cajun seasoning (97p for 108g from Asda) = 9p
1 tin of chopped tomatoes (31p Aldi) = 31p
1 stock cube to make 250ml stock (20p for 10 Tesco) = 2p
1 teaspoon of dried sage (49p 50g Aldi) = 1p

Grand total for 4 = £2.40

Method:

Heat any oil in a pan and add the chicken thighs (may have to do in batches) cook until browned and remove from the pan and set aside. Add the onion (chopped) garlic /celery (chopped) peppers and bay leaf to the pan and cook for 5 minutes, return the chicken to the pan – stir in the flour and Cajun seasoning cook for 30 seconds. Add the stock /tomatoes and sage – bring to the boil – then simmer for 10 minutes.

Best served with thick crusty bread (Aldi do a 500g packet mix to make your own 65p)

ENJOY!!!

Chili Con Carne

Ingredients:
225g Minced Beef (500g) steak mince Farmfoods = (£2.95
500g bag) = £1.47
1 onion = 10p
1/2 teaspoon hot chilli powder = 1p (49p ALDI 50g jar)
Tinned tomatoes 31p (Morrisons savers)
Kidney beans (Sweet Harvest Aldi) = 25p
2 bags boil in the bag rice (Bilash Aldi) – 29p
50g frozen mixed peppers (500g bag Farmfoods 66p – they
have 3 500g bags of any frozen veg for £2.00) = 6.5p

Grand total for 4 = £2.49

Method:
Heat any oil (or water) in a frying pan and add the chopped
onion (finely or roughly chopped). Add the beef mince and fry
for approximately 5 minutes then sprinkle over the chilli
powder and mix well. Stir in the tinned tomatoes reduce the
heat and simmer for approximately 30mins.
After about 15 minutes check the flavour and add seasoning
(salt and pepper) and more chilli powder if required. At this
time add the 2 bags of rice to boiling water and cook for 20
minutes.

After the last 15 minutes of chilli cooking time drain the
kidney beans and add to the mixture – cook for another 5
minutes at which time the rice will be ready. Serve and
ENJOY.

Corned Beef Hash

Ingredients:
500g old potatoes (13P) from the 7.5kg bag Farmfoods
1 onion (11P) bag of 7 = 79p (ALDI)
Stock pot 25p 4 for £1.00 (Home Bargains)
Tin of Corned beef £1.49 (ALDI)
(Total cost £1.97 – for 4) Optional tin of baked beans 18p Aldi

Method:
Cube the corned beef and chop the onion, Lightly sauté the onion in a little oil then when lightly browned add the corned beef. (I fried them together and the onions were a little underdone) Brown them both together then add to a bowl.

Cube the potatoes and add to boiling water with the stockpot – boil until soft then mash – adding a stockpot / a little butter and milk. Place the mash on the corned beef/onion or if you prefer mix it together then sprinkle a little grated cheese and brown under the grill.

ENJOY!!!

Turkey Mince Spaghetti Bolognaise

I much prefer to cook with turkey mince....it's got a lot less saturated fat than minced beef

Ingredients:
Packet of fresh turkey mince – 400g (1.99 Aldi) = £1.99
Onion (Farmfoods 79p for 14-15) = 5p
Half a jar of essentials pasta sauce (Aldi) 19p
Half a bulb of fresh garlic cloves (pack of 4 bulbs Farmfoods = 39p) 5p
2 teaspoons of oregano (49p for 50g jar at ALDI) 2p
2 teaspoons of paprika (49p for 50g jar at ALDI) 2p
350g dried spaghetti (23p for 500g at ALDI) 17p
2 tablespoons of tomato puree (35p concentrate ALDI) -1p

Total meal for 4 cost £2.50

Method:
I always dry fry my mince to keep the calories and saturated fat right down, so I add boiling hot water to my frying pan then add the whole packet of the turkey mince.
Get another pan going with boiling water ready to cook the spaghetti. Start to brown the turkey mince – stir in the tomato puree and add the oregano/paprika/and garlic.

Put the spaghetti in the boiling water and a tip add a splash of any oil to stop it sticking together. Add the chopped onion to the turkey mince and lightly fry-when all the turkey is browned and everything is mixed – add the pasta sauce – gently simmering until the spaghetti is cooked.

When the spaghetti is done drain and serve with the bolognaise sauce (and if the budget stretches add a sprinkle of parmesan and fresh basil leaves) season with black ground pepper and salt.
ENJOY

Chicken Saag with Boiled Rice

Ingredients:
2 onions (Farmfoods 79p bag 1.5kg) = 10p
4 garlic gloves (39p 4 bulbs Farmfoods) = 4p
2 teaspoons ginger (49p 50g Aldi) = 2p
1/2 tsp chilli (Lazy chilli Home Bargains 49p for a jar) = 1p
1 Tbsp ground coriander (50p supermarkets) = 3p
1/2 tsp turmeric = 1p
Drained well chopped tomatoes (34 p Aldi) = 34p...
300g defrosted chicken breast (£3.33 Farmfoods kilo bag) =
£1.15
150g natural (low fat) yoghurt (49p 500g pot Aldi) = 15p
1 tsp Garam Masala (50p 50g supermarkets) = 1p
100g defrosted and drained spinach (1kg bag Tesco = £1.40) =
14p
2 bags of boil in the bag rice (59p for 4 Aldi) = 30p

GRAND TOTAL FOR FAMILY OF 4 = £2.40

Method:
Heat any oil in a pan and add the chopped onion /chopped
garlic/ginger/lazy chilli /coriander and turmeric lightly fry for
about 2 minutes then add the chicken (chopped into small
pieces)

Put the rice on and cook until soft

Cook until the chicken is sealed and browned add the tomatoes
– cover and simmer for 20 minutes.
In a separate pan or microwave heat the spinach draining off
excess water. Turn off the heat and stir in the yoghurt/Garam
Masala and heated spinach....stir well and allow to stand for 5
minutes – then after this time – stir again and serve with the
cooked rice
and ...
ENJOY!!!!

Easy Chicken Risotto

Ingredients:

300g cooked shredded chicken (£3.33 Farmfoods 1kg) = 99p
226g Risotto Rice (£1.10 500g Asda/Tesco) = 55p
2 cloves of garlic (39p 4 bulbs Farmfoods) = 2p
50g leeks (66p 500g Farmfoods) = 6p
1 onion (79p 1.5kg bag Farmfoods) = 5p
2 tsps butter (500g £1.69 Aldi) = 2p
350 ml Chicken stock (10 for 20 p Tesco value) = 2p
150ml white wine (750ml Baron St Jean – Aldi £2.99) = 74p
200 ml water mixed with the wine
20g Frozen peas (1kg bag 99p Aldi) = 2p

Grand Total for 4 = £2.47

Sprinkle of parmesan 3p ;)

Method:

Preheat the oven to 180 degrees (fan) 200 non fan assisted
oven. Fry the chicken/onion/garlic/leeks/butter and rice mixing
in the buttery juices. Add the stock/ wine and water -season
with salt & pepper. Transfer to ovenproof dish and cook in the
oven for approx. 40 minutes (adding the peas after 35 minutes)
add extra stock / water if required.

Serve sprinkled with parmesan and...
ENJOY!!

Cheesy Fish Pie

Ingredients:
1/4 bag defrosted prawns (£2.99 From Aldi) = 70p
1/4 bag defrosted haddock (£2.99 from Aldi) = 70p
1 onion (79p bag from Aldi) = 10p
50g leeks (66p from Farmfoods 500g bag) = 6p
50g mushrooms (66p from Farmfoods 500g bag) = 6p
500g potatoes (7.5 kg bag £2.00 Farmfoods) = 10p
Cheese sauce serving (Bisto £1.25 granules makes 23 servings)
= 5p...
teaspoon butter = 5p
1 teaspoon dried tarragon (50g approx. 50p from
supermarkets) 1p
splash milk
5g cheese (£5.00 for 1kilo Farmfoods) = 5p
Fresh baguette – divided into 4 – approx. 50p from all
supermarkets

Grand total for 4 = £2.38

Method:
Boil the 500g potatoes and bring to a simmer.
Lightly fry the defrosted haddock in a little oil breaking it up
into small pieces, add the finely chopped onion add the
tarragon /leeks/mushrooms and prawns plus a little water –
heat through until all gently bubbling when the potatoes are
cooked drain the water add a splash of milk and the butter –
you may need a little more of both dependant on the
consistency, mash together.
Make up the cheese sauce and add to an ovenproof dish, add
the fish mixture and stir – coating everything in the cheese
sauce. (you may want to add a little extra milk as you don't
want it to be too dry)

Top with the mash and grate some cheese – grill for approx. 5mins until cheese has melted and browned then serve with the crusty baguette

ENJOY!!!!!

Teriyaki Chicken

Ingredients:
450g Chicken Breasts (£3.33 for a kilo FF) – £1.66
1/4 bottle of soy sauce (49p HB bottle) = 12p
2 tbsps Brown Sugar (79p for 500G Aldi) = 2p
1/2 teaspoon lazy ginger (49p jar HB) = 1p
2 tbsp white wine vinegar (80p 350 ml Asda) = 3p
1 clove garlic (39p 4 bulbs FF) = 1p
2 tbsp tomato ketchup (69p Aldi 563g) = 2p
1/2 packet dried noodles (49p full packet Aldi) = 25p
100g Stir fry veg (66p for 500g FF) = 12p

Grand total for 4 = £2.25

Method:
Mix all the ingredients together (apart from the
chicken/noodles and veg) to make a marinade. Add thinly
sliced chicken slices or chunks and make sure all the chicken is
covered and soaked in. Leave for approximately 30 minutes.

Boil the noodles and heat some oil in a frying pan or wok,
when very hot add the chicken and fry lightly, add in the stir
fry veg and the boiled drained noodles. Fry for a few more
minutes until everything is mixed together and covered in the
marinade – serve and ENJOY!!!!

Cottage Pie today

(One of my favourites (I cook it with turkey mince)

Ingredients:
1 tsp oil
2 finely chopped onions (79p 1.5kg FF) = 10p
2 Garlic cloves finely chopped (39p 4 bulbs FF) = 2p
675g Beef Mince (£2.50 800g FF) = £1.87
1 Tbsp plain flour (49p 1.5kg Aldi) = 1p
225mls Beef Stock with all-purpose seasoning added (20p for
10 Tesco) = 3p
2 Carrots Finely chopped (79p 1kg Aldi) = 10p
Few splashes of Worcester sauce
600g potatoes (7.5 kg £2.00 FF) = 12p

Grand total for a huge pie = £2.25

Serve with 200g Peas (1kg 99p Aldi) = 20p

TOTAL = £2.45

Method:
Preheat the oven to 180 degrees Fry onion and Garlic in a little
oil (or water as I do) when lightly browned add the meat .Add
the chopped carrots and season well. Stir in the flour (when the
meat is browned) and add stock then stir until thickened. Add a
few splashes of Worcs sauce (Optional – but makes it really
tasty) Transfer to an ovenproof casserole dish / tin and cook
for 1hour.

Boil the potatoes and make mash – after an hour put the mash
on the meat mixture and a sprinkle of cheese (optional) and
increase to 200 degrees then cook for another 20minutes until
the top is golden. Heat the peas and serve when cooked with
the cottage pie...
Then ENJOY!!!!!!

Chicken and Leek pie

Ingredients:
250g cooked chicken thighs /breasts torn into pieces (1kg bag
£3.33 Farm Foods) = 84p
300 ml chicken stock (10 for 20p Tesco value) = 2p
1 onion (79p bag 7-8 Aldi) = 10p
75ml white wine (Baron st Jean 750ml Aldi) = 30p
100g leeks (500g for 66p Farmfoods) = 13p
1 tbsp plain flour (49p 1.5kgs Aldi) = 2p
150 ml single cream (Tesco Creamfields 300ml) = 35p
1 tsp lemon juice (85p for 500ml Aldi) = 1p
2 tsp dried tarragon (supermarkets 50 p for 50g) = 2p
3/4 packet frozen shortcrust pastry (59p Herons/Cool Traders)
= 44p
splash milk for glaze

Grand Total for family of 4 = £2.24

Add 400g boiled potatoes for 10p (7.5kg Farm Foods) make
· mash if you prefer
100g peas = 10p (99p kilo bag Aldi) = 10p
£2.44

Method:
PREHEAT OVEN TO 180 Degrees
Cook the chicken as per the instructions. Then shred or chop to
small pieces.
Add 1 tsp any oil to a frying pan – add the chopped onion and
leeks and cook for 5 minutes, add the wine
then simmer for 5 minutes. Stir in the flour mix for 1 minute
then add the cream / stock and lemon juice. Add the chicken
and tarragon to the cream and leek mixture.

Transfer to a pie tin and cover with the pastry – trim the edges
then crimp with a fork or fingers – glaze with the milk and
bake for 30 – 35 minutes

Boil the potatoes to make the mash or just leave them boiled (nice with some all- purpose seasoning in) boil the peas near the end of the pie baking time.

ENJOY!!!!

Cornish pasties – made easy

Ingredients:
200g Swede (10p 100g from supermarkets) = 20p
300g potatoes (£2.00 7.5kg FF) = 6p
175g onion (79p 1.5kg FF) = 9p
300g Diced Beef steak (£2.50 45g FF) = £1.65
All- purpose seasoning / salt & Pepper
1 pack shortcrust pastry – defrosted (2 for £1.00 Lidl) = 50p

Grand total for 4 pasties = £2.50

Method:
Pre heat the oven 170 degrees (non- fan) 150 fan Gas 3

Peel potatoes /swede/onions and then dice into 1/4 cubes. Add
to the chopped meat – mix and season well with the all-
purpose seasoning/salt & pepper.

On a floured surface divide the dough into 4 pieces and roll
into a circle shape. Keep turning over the dough to prevent it
sticking.

When you have 4 circles place the meat mixture into half of
the circle and (add a little butter if required) fold over the
empty half and
seal the edges with either a fork or twisting with your fingers –
fold each end underneath. Glaze with a little milk.
Then bake for approx. 15mins or until golden brown.

ENJOY!!

Full English Carbonara (Plus a Veggie option)

Ingredients:
3 sausages (99p pack for 4 Aldi) = 40p (Or Quorn alternative)
100g smoked bacon (£1.00 for 200g FF) = 50p (or Quorn)
1 small onion (79p bag 15 FF) = 5p
1 garlic clove (39 for 4 bulbs FF) = 1p
150g mushrooms (66p 500g FF) = 15p
2 medium eggs and 1 egg yolk (99p for 6 Aldi) = 45p
2 ripe tomatoes – chopped (69p for 6 Aldi) = 15p
300g dried spaghetti (20p Aldi for 500g) = 12p
tbsp parmesan = 5p

(Or to make the dish even cheaper £1.38 omit the eggs and parmesan and add a serving of cheese sauce – Bisto 23p)

Grand Total For 4 = £1.88

Method:
Heat the pan with a little oil (or water) add chunks of sausage and cook for about 5 minutes – until browned, remove from the pan and leave to one side. Cook the pasta until tender – drain and leave a little water in the pan-whilst the pasta is cooking...

Pour off the fat from the pan and add the chopped bacon and fry for around a minute. Add chopped garlic and chopped onion – fry lightly and then add the mushrooms. Cover and lightly fry for a few minutes. Take the lid off add chopped tomatoes and cook until any juice has been absorbed.

Beat the eggs and parmesan and salt and pepper to taste then add to the spaghetti quickly to coat all the strands in the sauce

(or make up the cheese sauce and coat the spaghetti in it) add
the sausage and the bacon mixture – serve immediately.
ENJOY!!

Toad in the Hole (and Vegetarian alternative) Roast Potatoes/Peas and Gravy

Ingredients:
115g plain flour (49p 1.5kg Aldi) = 4p
1 pinch of salt
1 beaten egg (99p for 6 Free Range Aldi) = 15p
300ml milk (4 pints – 2 litres – Aldi 99p) = 15p
8 sausages Meat or Quorn (£1.00 Farmfoods) = £1.00
3 tbsp. any oil = 6p (any supermarket)
500g Potatoes (7.5kg £2.00 Farmfoods) = 15p
300g frozen peas (Aldi 1 kg 99p) = 3p
1 portion made gravy granules (75p for23 servings – Aldi) = 3p

Grand Total For 4 = £1.88

Method:
Make a batter by sifting the flour and salt into a bowl, make a well in the centre and add the beaten egg and half the milk. CAREFULLY stir the liquid into the flour until smooth – gradually beat in the rest of the milk and leave to stand for 30mins.
Boil the potatoes for approx. 10 minutes. Drain and leave to one side. Preheat the oven to 220 degrees.
Prick the sausages and place in a large ovenproof casserole dish add 1 tbsp. oil, cook in the oven for 10 minutes until beginning to
brown, and the fat is sizzling. Remove the sausages and quickly pour the batter over the sausages Return to the oven and cook for 35-45 minutes until the batter is well risen and golden brown.

Put the remaining oil in a separate baking tray and heat in the oven .When the oil in the baking tray is sizzling remove from the oven (when there is approx. 30mins cooking time left of the Toad in the Hole. Add the pre boiled potatoes and sprinkle with salt. Make sure the potatoes are well covered in the oil. Place back in the oven. (Occasionally turning over whilst cooking)

Approximately 5 minutes before the both dishes are due to leave the oven – Heat the peas and make up the gravy.

Remove the Toad in the hole and the potatoes – serve up with the peas and gravy – serve immediately and then

ENJOY!!!!!!!!!

Breakfast Pies

– favourites with kids (my husband makes these for students at work) .

Ingredients:
2 tins baked beans (24 p each Aldi) = 48p
6 rashers of bacon (£1.00 Farmfoods) = £1.00
6 Sausages (99p everyday essentials 99p Aldi) = 75p
500g potatoes (7.5kg £2.00 Farmfoods)) = 13p
1 stock cube 2p (20p for 10 Tesco) = 2p

splash of milk and bit of butter = max 5p

...

Grand Total for 4 people = £2.43

Method:
Boil the potatoes and stock cube.
Lightly fry the sausages – prick them first so they don't explode, when half cooked add the bacon (chopped first) Heat the beans and when the bacon sausage is cooked cut up the sausages and add to the beans along with the bacon. Mix altogether and keep simmering.
When the potatoes have boiled – mash with a little butter and milk. Put the sausage/bacon and beans into a suitable size dish and top with the mash (even grate a little cheese and grill) .

Then serve and ENJOY!!!!

Mexican Pork Casserole with boiled rice

Ingredients:
450g Pork Loin steaks (£15.00 for 5kg FF) = £1.35
¼ tsp ground cumin (48p Asda) – 1p
¼ tsp ground coriander (67p 100g Asda) = 1p
1 onion chopped (79p 1.5kg FF) = 5p
1 garlic clove crushed (39p 4 bulbs FF) = 1p
30g Plain flour (45p 1.5kg Aldi) = 1p
1 tbsp instant coffee (depends on brand) 3p
430ml veg stock plus all-purpose seasoning = 3p
50g mixed peppers (66p 500g FF) = 6p
1 tsp lazy chili (59p jar Home Bargains) = 1p
430g tin rinsed red kidney beans (23p Asda) = 23p
430g tin rinsed chick peas (37p Asda) – 37p
2 bags of boil in the bag rice (59p for 4 Aldi) = 30p

Grand Total = £2.47

Method:
Melt a little oil in a frying pan, add the defrosted sliced pork,
Fry until lightly browned. Add the cumin, coriander, garlic,
onion and flour fry for another 3-4 minutes then transfer to a
casserole dish. Dissolve the coffee into the hot stock and add
to the casserole stirring in well.
Add the peppers and cover. Transfer to a preheated oven (180
degrees) and cook for 40mins until the pork is tender. Add the
beans and chick peas and cook for a further 5 minutes – then
serve with the boiled rice.
ENJOY!!

Mozzarella Pasta with salad and garlic baguette

Ingredients:
1 onion (79p 1.5 kg FF) = 5p
2 cloves garlic (39p 4 bulbs FF) = 2p
1 tbsp tomato puree (35p 200g Aldi) = 5p
400g tin chopped tomatoes (34p Aldi) = 34p
125g Mozzarella (light or full fat 44p Aldi) = 44p
500g penne pasta (29p Aldi 500g) – 29p
10g Parmesan (200g £2.50 Asda) = 12p
½ packet prepared salad (49p bag Aldi) = 25p
150g cherry tomatoes (49p 300g Aldi) = 25p
½ cucumber chopped finely (50p full one Aldi) = 25p
2 tbsps chopped fresh basil (living pot – therefore can be used
more times 89p Aldi) = 10p
Full garlic baguette (34p Aldi) = 34p

Grand Total = £2.50

Method:
Heat a little oil in a pan, fry the onion and garlic. Cover for 10
mins (simmer) until soft, add the puree and cook for a minute.
Stir in the tomatoes and season with s & p. Simmer for 25
minutes and then add the chopped mozzarella stir until melted
through.
Approximately 15 minutes before the end of the tomato /
mozzarella cooking time – boil the pasta until soft – drain and
when the tomato and mozzarella is cooked add the tomato
mixture and stir through.
Sprinkle the parmesan on the pasta mixture and a little on the
prepared salad, then serve altogether with the garlic bread and
ENJOY!

Vegetarian Glamorgan Sausages with mash and Leeks

Ingredients:

150g grated Caerphilly cheese (180g £1.00 Asda) = 83p
200g Fresh white breadcrumbs (55p 800g Aldi) = 13p
3 spring onions (50p bunch Asda) = 15p
1 tbsp parsley (49p jar Aldi) = 1p
1 tbsp thyme (49p jar Aldi) = 1p
3 eggs – 1 separated (95p 6 free range Aldi) = 47p
100g defrosted leeks (66p 500g FF) = 13p
500g potatoes (7.5kg £2.00 FF) = 10p
Bisto veg granules (£1.00 makes 23 servings Asda) = 3p
Milk and butter to make the mash

Grand Total = £1.85

Method:

Boil the potatoes to make mash.
Preheat the oven to 140 degrees (120 fan assisted) mix the
cheese with 150g breadcrumbs/chopped spring onions and
herbs in a large bowl season well. Add the 2 whole eggs and
extra yolk. Mix well combining all ingredients, then chill for 5
minutes. Lightly beat the egg white in a bowl and tip the rest
of the breadcrumbs on a plate. Take 2 tbsps of the cheese
mixture and roll into the shape of a sausage approx. 1 ½ inches
long. Roll in the egg white then in the breadcrumbs to coat.
Repeat to make approx. 12 sausages. Heat a little oil in a pan
and fry in batched for 6 -8 minutes. Keeping them warm in the
preheated oven.
Take the boiled potatoes to make mash adding a little butter
and milk until smooth. Sautee the leeks in a little butter. Serve
the mash /leeks and sausages with the made up gravy and
ENJOY!

Tartiflette (potato, cheese & bacon Gratin)

Ingredients:
1 kg sliced potatoes (7.5kg £2.00 FF) = 20p
3 garlic cloves – kept whole (39p for 4 bulbs FF) = 3p
125g Bacon lardons (89p 150g Aldi) = 75p
2 tbsp thyme (49p jar Aldi) = 5p
300ml Crème Fraiche (69p 300ml Aldi) = 69p
100g Camembert cheese (250g £1.39 Aldi) – 70p

Grand total = £2.42

Method:
Preheat the oven to 180 degrees. Cook the potato slices in boiling water until just tender – drain. Heat oil in a large frying pan and add the whole cloves and bacon – cook for 3-4 mins, then gently add the potato slices then cook for a further 3-4 minutes. Pour in the crème fraiche and thyme then cover the potato mixture.
Transfer to a casserole dish and cover with the camembert then bake for 20mins.

Low Fat Chicken Mulligatawny stew with crusty bread

Ingredients:
2 onions (79p 1.5kg FF) = 10p
4 carrots – approx. 100g (59p 1 kg Aldi) = 6p
300g thinly sliced chicken breasts (1kg £3.00 FF) = 99p
4 garlic cloves (39p for 4 bulbs FF) = 4p
2 tbsps mild curry powder = 2p
2 tbsps tomato puree (35p 200g Aldi) = 5p
2 tbsps Mango chutney (370g Aldi 89p) = 7p
5 ¼ pints chicken stock pot with all-purpose seasoning (99p
for 6 Home Bargains) = 18p
125g White rice (59p for 4 bags Aldi) = 15p
1 packet crusty bread mix (65p Aldi) = 65p

Grand total = £2.31

Method:
Fry the chopped onions, add the carrots and cook for about 3
minutes until tender. Add thinly sliced chicken and chopped
garlic cook for a further 3-5 minutes.
Stir in the curry powder, tomato puree and mango chutney,
cook for about 1 minute, add the stock and rice and bring to
the boil then simmer for about 20minutes until the rice is
cooked and the veg is tender. Serve with the crusty bread
(made up as per instructions on the packet)
Enjoy!!

Chicken pie with sweet potato mash

Ingredients:

600g Sweet potatoes (69p 750g Aldi) = 55p
3 tbsp plain flour (1.5kg 45p Aldi) = 3p
2 garlic cloves (39p 4 bulbs FF) = 2p
1 onion (1.5kg 79p FF) = 5p
200g mushrooms (66p 500g FF) = 26p
1 chicken stock cube with all-purpose seasoning = 3p
400g chicken (£13.00 5kg FF) = £1.20
40g butter (250g 98p Aldi) = 15p
1 sprig rosemary (31g 70p Asda) = 10p
2 tbsp tomato puree (35p 200g Aldi) = 5p

Grand Total = £2.44

Method:

Coat the chicken in the flour, heat a little oil in a pan and brown the chicken, then set aside. Heat a little more oil in the pan and add the garlic onion and mushrooms cook for 5 minutes. Return the chicken to the pan and add the stock cube, puree ,rosemary and 250ml cold water. Bring to the boil and simmer for 30minutes – stirring occasionally.
Meanwhile preheat the oven to 200degrees (180 fan) cook the sweet potatoes in a boiling water for 10 mins until tender.
Mash with the butter and a little milk, season well.
Spoon the chicken mixture into a casserole dish and remove the rosemary sprig. Top the chicken mixture with the mash and bake for 25mins until browned.
Serve and ENJOY!!

Thai Turkey & Chili Burgers

Ingredients:
300g turkey mince (450g £1.99 Aldi) = £1.32
Packet of bread mix (65p Aldi makes 10 rolls) = 26p
Sweet Chili sauce (Healthy boy Morrisons 700ml £1.19) = 2p
1 tsp lazy ginger (jar 59p Home Bargains) = 1p
1 garlic clove minced finely (39p 4 bulbs Farmfoods) = 1p
4 spring onions finely chopped (45p bunch approx. 10 Aldi) =
18p
Few leaves of fresh coriander (living pot 49p Aldi) = 5p
4 tbsps Mayonnaise (40p Aldi 500ml) = 2p
Lime zest (39p for 3 Aldi super 6) = 13p
Salad to garnish:
¼ cucumber (39p whole one Aldi) = 10p
¼ lettuce (45p whole one Aldi) = 11p
2 tomatoes (39p for 6 Aldi) = 13p

Grand Total = £2.34

Method:
Mix minced turkey, 2 tbsp chili sauce, ginger, garlic and lime
zest, spring onions, coriander and season with salt & pepper
until well combined. Shape the mixture into 4 burger shapes
(the mix will be quite wet but will make juicy burgers) Under a
preheated grill – grill the burgers for 6 – 7 mins each side until
cooked through.
Make up the bread buns as per the packet (may have to be in
advance of making the burgers)
Add the burgers to the cooled sliced buns. Add a little more
coriander to the mayo, add lettuce tomato and cucumber to
each burger and add the mayo to each burger and drizzle the
remaining chili sauce over the top.
Low fat and tasty! Then ENJOY!!

Tuna and sweetcorn fishcakes with Herby Wedges

Ingredients:
450g boiled cubed potatoes (7.5kg £2.00 Farmfoods) = 9p
2 tbsp mayo (500mls 40p Aldi) = 1p
2 x 185g tins tuna (75p tin Aldi) = £1.50
200g Sweetcorn defrosted (66p 500g Farmfoods) = 26p
1 tsp parsley (49p jar or living pot Aldi) = 1p
1 egg (95p for 6 free range Aldi) = 15p
2 tsp Chives (49p Aldi) = 5p
100g fresh breadcrumbs (800g loaf 55p Aldi) = 7p
For the Wedges
400g potatoes (as above) = 8p cut into wedges
4 garlic cloves (as above) = 4p
½ tsp oregano (49p jar Aldi) = 1p
½ tsp paprika (49p jar Aldi) = 1p
½ tsp thyme (49p jar Aldi) = 1p
½ tsp black pepper = 1p
1 tsp salt less than 1p
Fry light or olive oil (price depends on oil but pennies)
100g frozen peas cooked (1kg 99p Aldi) – 10p

Grand Total = £2.41

Method:
For the wedges:
Preheat the oven to 220 degrees and line a large roasting tray with foil. Cut each (washed but skin on) potato into wedges and place in a large mixing bowl. Add the rest of the ingredients and fully coat all the wedges.
Place them on the tray and cook for 35-40 minutes until crispy (keep giving them a shake) .
For the fishcakes:
Boil the potatoes and when tender and allow to steam dry in a colander. Mash in a bowl with a little milk and season. Stir in

the mayo, drained tuna, defrosted sweetcorn and the snipped chives mix thoroughly and shapes into 4 patties, then chill until firm. Dip each patty into the beaten egg and coat in the breadcrumbs chill again for 15 minutes when you have done all 4. Fry in a little oil for 2-3 minutes each side and then serve with the wedges and peas...

Jamaican Jerk chicken and Potato with corn on the cob

Ingredients:
400g potatoes (7.5kg £2.00 Farmfoods) = 8p
250g chicken (5kg £15.00 FF) = 75p
100g peppers (66p 500g FF) – 16p
1 tbsp jerk seasoning (100g 69p Tesco) = 1p
¼ tin pineapple rings (432g 55p Aldi) = 14p
4 frozen corn on the cob (£1.44 for 8 Asda) = 72p

Grand Total = £1.86

Method:
Cook the corn on the cob as per instructions.
Boil the potatoes until tender and drain thoroughly. Meanwhile heat a little oil in a frying pan and stir fry the thinly sliced chicken, peppers and jerk seasoning for about 5 minutes. Add the pineapple rings and 2 tbsp of the pineapple juice then add the potatoes. Stir fry again for 1-2 minutes and then serve with the corn on the cob.
ENJOY!!

Chorizo and Potato Spanish omelette

Ingredients:

6 eggs (95p 6 free range Aldi) = 95p
1 red onion (1kg 69p Aldi) = 6p
300g New potatoes sliced and boiled until tender (69p 750g
Aldi) = 28p
100g sliced chorizo (Tesco Deli counter 100g 90p) = 90p
2 tbsp fresh parsley (49p living pot Aldi) = 4p

Grand Total = £2.23

Method:

Heat a little oil in a pan – add the potatoes and onion and cook
for 5 mins until onion is soft. Add the chorizo and fry for
another 5 minutes. Preheat the grill to medium. Crack the eggs
in a bowl, season and add the parsley. Add to the pan and cook
for 5 minutes – then heat under the grill until set and golden.
Garnish with a little more parsley.
ENJOY!!

Spicy Turkey Bhuna with boiled rice

Ingredients:
1 onion (1.5kg 79p FF) = 5p
2 garlic cloves chopped (39p 4 bulbs FF) = 2p
1 tsp lazy ginger (59p Home Bargains jar) = 1p
250g diced turkey £2.59 375g Aldi) = £1.72
2 bags boil in the bag rice (59p 4 bags Aldi) = 30p
1 tin tomatoes (31p Aldi) = 31p
1tsp fennel seeds (69p 100g Asda) = 1p
½ tsp cumin (48p jar Asda) – 1p
1 tsp ground coriander (100g 67p Asda) = 1p
2 sprigs thyme (31g 70p Asda) = 3p

Grand Total £2.47

Method:
Preheat a non-stick pan until hot, add the onion, garlic, ginger, fennel, and spices and cook until lightly browned. Add the turkey and seal until browned. Add the tinned tomatoes and the thyme and then simmer for 20 minutes then serve with the cooked boiled rice.
ENJOY!!

Mexican baked eggs Arriba with Tacos

Ingredients:
75g Chorizo (90p 100g Tesco Deli) = 67p
1 onion (1.5kg 79p FF) = 5p
1 courgette (89p 3 Aldi) = 30p
1 tin tomatoes (31p Aldi) = 31p
100g mixed peppers (500g 66p FF) = 13p
4 eggs (95p for 6 free range) = 63p
4 Taco shells (24 for £2.50 Asda) – 41p

Grand Total = £2.50

Method:
Fry the chorizo in a pan until the fat starts to run. Add the chopped onion and courgette, stir for around 5 minutes until the veg are soft. Add the peppers and tomatoes – stir for 2-3 minutes. Make 4 spaces in the mixture and crack in the eggs then cook gently over a low heat for 6-8 mins until the eggs are cooked to your liking. Serve with the tacos and ENJOY!!

Courgette, Tomato and Cheese Gratin

Ingredients:
2 onions (79p 1.5 kg FF) = 10p
2 garlic cloves (39p 4 bulbs FF) = 2p
3 courgettes (89p 3 Aldi) = 89p
250g Plum tomatoes (75p 250g Aldi) = 75p
50g Breadcrumbs (800g loaf 55p Aldi) = 3p
50g Olives (230g 45p Aldi) 10p
110g Cheddar (450g Aldi Everyday essentials) = 48p
3 stems tarragon (70p approx. 20 stems Asda) = 10p

Grand Total = £2.47

Method:
Preheat the oven to 200 degrees. In a frying pan add a little water and fry the chopped onion and garlic. Remove the onions and put in a casserole dish and season. Add a little more water to the pan and add the sliced courgettes and stir until cooked and starting to brown, add these to the casserole dish and scatter over the olives and tarragon leaves. Then add the sliced plum tomatoes. Mix together the breadcrumbs and grated cheese and sprinkle over the veg. Cover with foil and cook for 20 mins. Remove the foil and cook for another 10 minutes allowing the top to brown.
ENJOY!!

Polenta with Saucy Mushrooms

Ingredients:
75g Pancetta cubes (130g £1.50 Tesco) = 86p
100g polenta (500g Morrisons 79p) = 16p
2 garlic cloves (39p 4 bulbs Farmfoods) = 2p
½ tin tomatoes (31p Aldi) = 16p
1 tbsp sun dried tomato paste (80g 72p Morrisons) = 5p
400ml milk (4 pints £1 most supermarkets) = 20p
2 tbsp basil (living pot 49p Aldi_) = 5p
40g Parmesan (£1.29 100g Morrisons) = 51p
175g mushrooms washed and halved (89p 350g Aldi) = 45p

Grand Total = £2.46

Method:
Fry the pancetta for 2 minutes add the mushrooms and garlic
then fry for another 2 minutes, Add the tomatoes and paste and
basil then cover and simmer for 10 minutes.
Meanwhile heat the milk in a pan when it comes to the boil
add the polenta and cook until thickened, remove from the heat
– season and add the parmesan.
Serve the mushroom mixture over the polenta and garnish with
fresh basil leaves.
ENJOY!!

Pasta and Bean stew with tortilla chips

Ingredients:
1 onion (1.5 kg 79p FF) = 5p
1 carrot (1kg 69p Aldi) = 10p
50g Bacon rashers (250g £1.25 Aldi) = 25p
2 celery sticks (69p approx. 10 Aldi) _ = 13p
2 garlic cloves (39p 4 bulbs FF) – 2p
2 pints stock with all-purpose seasoning = 3p
1 tin of tomatoes (31p Aldi) = 31p
65g Conchiglie pasta (500g 49p Aldi) = 6p
1 tin mixed beans (62p Asda) = 62p
100g Green beans (66p 500g FF) = 13p
1 Courgette (89p 4 Aldi) = 30p
1 packet everyday essentials Tortilla chips = 46p

Grand Total = £2.46

Method:
Heat a little oil in a pan and fry the chopped onion and
chopped bacon for 3 minutes, stir in the chopped celery,
chopped carrot and chopped garlic and cook for 3 minutes, add
the stock and tomatoes and bring to the boil, add the pasta and
cook for 8 minutes.
Stir in the mixed beans, green beans and courgette and simmer
for about 5 minutes until the pasta and veg are soft. Either
sprinkle crushed tortilla chips over or whole and serve then
ENJOY!!

Corned Beef and Egg Hash

Ingredients:
25g butter (98p 250g Aldi) = 9p
1 onion (79p 1.5 kg FF) = 5p
50g mixed peppers (500g 66p FF) = 6p
100g diced boiled potatoes (7.5kg £2.00 FF) = 1p
1 tin corned beef (£1.49 Aldi) = £1.49
¼ tsp paprika (49p jar Aldi) = 1p
4 eggs (95p 6 free range Aldi) = 63p
Tomato ketchup (69p 563g Aldi) price depends on how much
you serve with.

Grand Total = £2.34

Method:
Heat the butter in a pan and add the chopped onion fry for 5-6
minutes. In a bowl mix together the peppers, potatoes, diced
corned beef, paprika and season. Add this to the pan and press
down gently to distribute over the onion. Stir for about 3-4
mins until a crust forms / stir this and then let another crust
form – do this until mix is well browned. Make 4 wells in the
pan and crack in the eggs and cook until the eggs are set. Then
serve with tomato ketchup.
ENJOY!!

Slow Cooker – Cowboy Pie

Ingredients:
500g Minced beef & onion (800g bag Farmfoods 2 for £5.00)
= £1.56
2 Tablespoons Worcester sauce = max 5p
1 tin baked beans (24 p Aldi) = 24p
1 bay leaf (49p box Aldi) = 1p
200ml beef stick (20p for 10p Tesco Value range) – 2p
750g potatoes (7.5 kg £2.00 – Farmfoods) = 15p
Splash of milk and butter to make mash.
Cheese sprinkle if required.

Grand total for 4 = £2.03

Method:
Preheat the slow cooker. Fry the minced beef and onion with
water or oil if preferred, add the Worcester sauce and baked
beans, the bay leaf and stock, add salt & pepper then when
gently bubbling spoon into the slow cooker pot and cook for 7
– 8 hours.

Top with the mash then if required add cheese and brown
under the grill until browned.

Serve and
ENJOY!!!

Slow Cooker Kheema Mutter

Ingredients:
400g Minced beef & onion (800g £2.00 Farmfoods 2 bags for £4.00) = £1.25

2 garlic cloves (39 p 4 bulbs Farmfoods) = 2p

2 tbsp. curry powder (to suit your taste) = 3p

1 tsp lazy ginger (59p jar Home Bargains) = 1p

1/4 tsp ground turmeric (50p 50g jar from most supermarkets) = 1p

1/2 onion (79p bag of 7 -8 Aldi) = 5p

1 tsp lazy chili (59p jar Home Bargains) = 1p

1 tin drained chopped tomatoes (34p Aldi) = 34p

200 ml coconut milk (50p 400ml tin Asda) = 25p

4 tablespoons fresh chopped Coriander (49p Fresh herbs Aldi) = 12p (1/4 pack)

100g frozen peas (1kg Aldi 99p) = 10p

2 bags boil in the bag rice (59p for 4 Aldi) = 30p

Grand total for 4 = £2.49

Method:
Put the Beef mince /garlic/ginger/curry powder and turmeric in a bowl and mix with a little salt – using your fingers.

heat water in a frying pan and add the onion and chili fry for around a minute then add the beef mixture and fry for around 2 – 3 minutes.

Transfer to the slow cooker and add the tomatoes and coconut milk and peas. Cover with the lid and cook for 6-8 hours on a low heat.

when home boil the rice and when cooked serve with the Kheema Mutter – sprinkle with chopped coriander serve and...
ENJOY!!!

Cheese & onion pies

Preheat the oven to 180 degrees

Ingredients:
500g potatoes (7.5 kg £2.00 Farmfoods) = 13p
3 onions (79 p for 7-8 Aldi) = 30p
200g grated cheese (1kg Farmfoods £5.00) = £1.00
1 stock cube (10 for 20p Tesco) = 2p
1 tsp butter 2p...
100g peas – (1kg bag from Aldi 99p) = 10p

GRAND TOTAL for 4 = £1.57

Method:
Boil potatoes until soft in the stock and make mash (with a little butter and milk) Sautee finely chopped onions in a little butter until soft.

Layer in 4 small pots Mash/Cheese/Onion building layers until all gone and make sure the last layer is cheese – to form a crunchy topping.

Bake for approx. 20 mins and serve with cooked peas then...

ENJOY!!!!

Aubergine and Tomato bake with Jacket Potatoes

Ingredients:

2 Medium Aubergines (69p each Lidl) = £1.38
3 cloves garlic (39p 4 bulbs Farmfoods) = 3p
1 3/4 tins plum tomatoes (34p tin Aldi) = 60p
1 packet Mozarella (44p Aldi – same price for
Low fat mozzarella and tastes just the same) = 44p
1 tsp oregano and 3 slices of stale breadcrumbs (mix together)
= 1p
4 potatoes up to 400g (7.5kg £2.00 Farmfoods) = 4p to make
jacket potatoes.

Grand total £2.50 for 4 people.

Method:

Preheat the oven to 190 degs or 170 for fan assisted. Heat 1
tbsp. of any oil in a frying pan and add the seasoned
aubergines (sliced into rounds) and fry until golden.
Remove from the pan and fry garlic and add the tomatoes –
season again
Layer the Aubergine /mozzarella/tomatoes in a baking dish –
cover with the breadcrumb/oregano mixture – bake for approx.
25 mins or until golden and bubbling. Make the Jacket
potatoes – either in the Microwave or as I prefer slowly in the
oven. Serve the bake over the jacket potatoes and then...

ENJOY!!

Low fat Finger Lickin Chicken

Ingredients:
325g Chicken drumsticks (750g £1.99 Aldi) = 99p
6 tbsps Soy Sauce (Aldi 150ml 59p) = 3p
2 tsps Chili flakes (East end Tesco 75g 99p) = 2p
2 tsps lazy ginger (59p jar Home Bargains) = 2p
2 tsp tomato puree (35p tube of concentrate Aldi) = 2p
2 tsp Sweetener (89p 75g Aldi) = 2p
4 Corn on the Cob (£1.44 for 8 frozen Asda) = 72p
4 garlic cloves (39p 4bulbs FF) = 4p
350g New potatoes (85p 750g Aldi) = 39p

Grand Total for 4 = £2.25

Method:
Place the defrosted corn in foil and spray with light cooking spray (if you have any – if not will steam anyway) add the chopped garlic cloves (optional) to each cob.
Place the drumsticks in an ovenproof dish and mix the rest of the ingredients together and cover the chicken. Marinate for around 20 mins in the fridge.
Meanwhile preheat the oven to 190 (170 assisted) and cook the chicken (still covered in the sauce) and the sweetcorn for around 30-35 mins until the chicken juice runs clear.
Serve with boiled potatoes/sweetcorn and any juices left over from the marinade can be used as a dipping sauce.

Low fat Fish & Chip Pie

Ingredients:
370g Basa fillets – or any white fish fillets (400 £1.99 Aldi) = £1.84
25g Sauce Flour (Carrs 500g bag Tesco 62p) = 3p
300ml semi skimmed milk (£1.60 8 pints FF) = 12p
100g frozen peas (1kg 99p Aldi) = 10p
400g potatoes (7.5kg £2.00 FF) = 4p
2 tsps lemon juice = 2p
2 tsps oil (price depends on oil)
1 tsp All Purpose seasoning = 1p

Grand Total for 4 = £2.15

Method:
Preheat the oven to 200 degrees.
Prepare the potatoes – peel / wash and chop into chipsticks – then par boil in boiled water and the A/P seasoning.
Steam/poach the fish (in a little milk) for approx 8 – 10 mins until white.
Put the cornflour and milk in a saucepan and bring to the boil stirring gently until a sauce is formed, then simmer for 5 minutes.
Mix the chipsticks, lemon juice and oil for the topping.
Flake the fish ,add peas and sauce and season with S&P. Place in a shallow ovenproof dish, top with the chips – add a little more seasoning then cook until the chips are brown and crisp.
(cook uncovered)
Then ENJOY!!!!

Simple Vegetable Curry – with boiled rice

Ingredients:
1 onion chopped (79p bag Aldi for 7-8) = 10p
2 garlic cloves chopped (39p 4 bulbs Farmfoods) = 2p...
2 tbsps. curry powder mild- hot dependent on your palate! = 5p
1/2 teaspoon lazy chili (49p jar Home Bargains) = 1p
175g peas (Aldi 99p for 1kg) − 17p
250g carrots (1kg bag 79p Aldi) = 19p
2 courgettes (3 for £1.29 Aldi) = 86p
125g mushrooms (66p 500g Farmfoods) = 16p
200g peeled potatoes and cubed (7.5kg bag £2.00 Farmfoods) = 5p
Tin of chopped tomatoes (34p Aldi) = 34p
100g mixed peppers (66p 500g Farmfoods) = 13p
2 bags of boil in the bag rice (59p for 4 bags Aldi) = 30p

Grand total for 4 is £2.38

Method:
Fry the onion and garlic/chili then add the curry powder. Add the Prepared veg – carrots / courgettes/potatoes
add the tinned tomatoes and then simmer for 30mins – at this point then add the frozen pepper/peas and mushrooms and simmer for a further 10 mins. (my tip is to make the day before you want to eat it – curry always tastes better the day after its made as it soaks in all the flavours)
Serve with cooked boiled rice.

ENJOY!

Spanish Omelette

Ingredients:
280g Potatoes thinly sliced (£2.00 7.5kg FF) = 6p
2 cloves garlic (39p FF for 4 bulbs) = 2p
5 medium Free Range eggs (Aldi 99p for 6) = 90p
2 onions thinly sliced (79p for approx. 15 – FF) = 10p
110g Frozen peas (99p 1 kg Aldi) = 11p
2 salad tomatoes (Aldi 79p for 6) = 26p
sprinkle of paprika / salt and pepper to taste.
Grating of cheese (optional) cost depends on the cheese

£1.35 GRAND TOTAL which will serve 4 people.

Serve with Rice 30p 2 bags boil in the bag rice (Aldi) or…
Essentials mixed salad 49p Aldi or…
Garlic baguette 34p Aldi

Or even with all 3 will come in at £2.48 for 4 people!!

Method:
Heat a little oil (any) in a large frying pan add the potato slices
to the bottom – sprinkle on some salt and then cook on a
medium heat until tender, remove & drain off extra oil.
Whisk the eggs in a bowl / jug and add the paprika, add the
chopped onion / garlic and potatoes to the egg mixture, add
some more oil to the pan and then make it very hot. Add the
egg mixture and keep shaking the pan until 1/2 set. Add the
peas at this point.

Put a plate over the pan and tip upside down and then put the
uncooked side back in the pan. (Or if you prefer grill it.)
sprinkle on a little cheese if required. Then serve with
whatever you choose!!

ENJOY!!

Slow Cooker Mushroom & Tomato Curry

Ingredients:
4 cloves garlic (4 bulbs 39p Farmfoods) = 4p
2 teaspoons ginger (59p Lazy ginger Home Bargains) = 2p
1 finely chopped onion (79p bag from Aldi) = 10p
1 tbsp. curry powder (strength dependant on taste) = 2p
3 tbsp. water = free
400g button mushrooms (£1.00 – Asda) 100 ml
Coconut milk (49p Asda 400 ml) = 13p
1 tin of chopped tomatoes – drained well (34P – Aldi) = 34p
1/4 bunch fresh coriander (49p 25p Aldi fresh bag-freeze the
rest) = 10p
2bags boil in the bag rice (59p for 4 Aldi) = 30p

GRAND TOTAL FOR = £2.05

Method:
Blend garlic /ginger/onion/curry powder and water in a blender
or food
processor (If you don't have one chop as finely as you can – or
Argos do a hand one for under £5.00).
Fry the Mushrooms in a little oil or water for 4 – 5 mins,
remove and then fry the onion mixture for 3-4 mins.
Transfer the mushrooms/onion mixture/coconut milk and
tomatoes – season well
and then cook for 4-6 hours on a high heat or longer on a lower
heat.

Boil the rice and serve with chopped fresh coriander …
ENJOY!!

Greek Dolmas & Pitta Breads

Ingredients:
200g Minced Beef (800g £2.50 – 4 FF) = 62p
I onion peeled and chopped = 5p
50g mushrooms (66p 500g FF) = 6p
1 Tomato skinned and finely chopped (49p Aldi salad fresh)
10p
1 tsp oregano 1p
1 Tbsp tomato puree (concentrate Aldi 34p) = 5p
salt & pepper ...
8 Savoy Cabbage leaves (69p for full cabbage Aldi) = 35p
(half Cabbage)
250ml tomato juice (63p litre Tesco) = 16p
1 tsp cornflour = 1p
splash Worcs sauce = 3p
1 tbsp freshly chopped mint 49p pack Aldi) = 5p
1 bag boil in the bag rice (59p for 4 bags Aldi) = 15p
4 pitta breads (pack of 6 49p Aldi) = 32p
3/4 pot Houmous (65p Aldi) = 49p
1 tbsp. mint leave (49p pack Aldi) = 5p

GRAND TOTAL – £2.50 for 4 people.

Preheat the Oven to 180degrees non assisted and 160 assisted.

Method:
In a non-stick pan cook the minced beef/onion/mushrooms and
(cooked) rice for around 4 minutes. Stir in the tomato/oregano
and tomato puree. Season to taste. Blanch the cabbage leaves
in boiling water – then divide the meat mixture in the cabbage
leaves and roll up – hold in place with a cocktail stick if you
want to.

Blend the tomato juice and cornflour – place in a small pan
and bring to the boil, Add worcs sauce and chopped mint, and

pour half the sauce into an ovenproof dish and arrange the
stuffed leaves over the top and then bake for 1 hour.

Warm the remaining sauce and when baked pour over the
leaves – serve with warmed pitta bread and houmous – and…
ENJOY !

Pesto Chicken & Roasted Veg

Ingredients:
500g Potatoes, peeled and halved (7.5 kg £2.00 FF) = 10p
1 red pepper (3 for 89p Aldi) = 29p
200g cherry tomatoes (£1.29 punnet Aldi) = 50p
1 1/2 courgettes (£1.29 for 4 Aldi) = 47p
3 garlic cloves (39 p for 4 bulbs FF) = 3p
1 tsp Rosemary = 1p
1 tsp thyme – 1p
300g Chicken Breasts-defrosted (1kg = £3.33) 99p
1 onion (1.5kg 79p FF) = 5p
2 tsps. pesto (79p jar Aldi) = 5p

Grand Total for 4 = £2.50

Method:
Preheat the oven to 200 degrees /place potatoes in a (lightly oiled) ovenproof dish and cook for 20mins. Add the pepper (chopped) tomatoes/cut courgettes garlic and herbs – return to the oven and cook for another 20mins.

Heat a little oil in a pan and add the sliced chicken fry for 8-10 mins. Just before the end of the cooking time add the pesto. When the veg are cooked add the pesto chicken – mixing well and then serve immediately.

ENJOY

Low Fat Hungarian Pork with Peppers

Ingredients:
4 Pork Chops (£3.33 for 8 FF) = £1.66
4 tsp smoked paprika (49p 50g jar Aldi) = 4p
3 onions (1.5kg bag 79p FF) = 15p
4 cloves garlic (39p 4 bulbs FF) = 4p
150g Frozen peppers (66p for 500g FF) = 20p
500ml hot chicken stock mixed with All Purpose seasoning) =
3p
75g frozen peas (99p kilo bag Aldi) = 8p
2 bags boil in bag rice (59p for 4 Aldi) = 30p
Salt and pepper to season.

GRAND TOTAL FOR 4 = £2.50

Method:
Season the defrosted pork chops with salt, pepper and dusting
of paprika. Put a little water (or oil) in a large sided lidded
frying pan and heat until hot then add the chops, cook for
approx. 5 mins until golden. Remove and set aside.

Fry the chopped onions /garlic and peppers until soft Reduce
the heat / add the stock and return the chops on top of the
peppers mixture. Return to the boil then and simmer for
15mins until the chops are cooked through.

Boil the rice according to the instructions (I like to boil in a
little all- purpose seasoning. Just before cooked boil the peas in
a separate pan or heat in the microwave. Remove the rice from
the bags and mix in the peas. Serve the chops over the rice and
peas – with the peppers / onions and juices. Season to taste.
ENJOY!!

Chicken and sweetcorn soup

Ingredients:
1 large chicken breast = 33p (£3.33 Farmfoods)
1 stock cube (20p for 10 Tesco) = 2p all some all- purpose seasoning make up 500 ml stock.
1 garlic clove 1p
200g sweetcorn (Farmfoods 500g bag 66p) = 13p
2 tbsp. cornflour dissolved in water – max 5p
1 egg = 16p (6 Free Range Aldi = 99p)

Grand total = 70p

Method:
Place the chicken in a pan and cover with the water season (salt n pepper) boil for 10 minutes. Drain and cut into strips – leave to one side.
Pour stock into the pot and add the garlic and sweetcorn. Add the chicken strips and gradually stir in the cornflour mixture as it begins to simmer. After 1 minute pour in the beaten egg and cook for a further 1 minute stirring with a fork to break the egg pieces.

Season and serve immediately

ENJOY!!!!

Tex Mex Jacket Potatoes with Chilli

Ingredients:
4 large baking Potatoes (99p for 4 Aldi) = 99p
1 crushed garlic clove (39p 4 bulbs Farmfoods) = 1p
1 onion (79p 1.5 kg Farmfoods) = 5p
50g mixed peppers (66p 500g Farmfoods) = 6p
225g Minced beef (£2.69 750g Aldi) = 80p
¼ tsp lazy chili (49p jar Home Bargains) = 1p
1tsp ground cumin (49p jar Aldi) = 1p
Pinch cayenne pepper (78p jar Asda) = 1p
200g tinned chopped tomatoes (33p Aldi) = 16p
2 tbsp tomato paste (35p 200ml tube concentrate Aldi) = 5p
½ tsp oregano (49p jar Aldi) = 1p
½ tsp marjoram (35p 8g Tesco) = 1p
½ tin of drained kidney beans (25p Aldi) = 13p
1 tbsp chopped coriander (49p fresh bag Aldi) = 2p
60ml soured cream to serve (300ml 79p Aldi) = 15p
Grand Total: £2.47

Method:
Preheat the oven to 220 degrees and pierce the potatoes cook
for 30 minutes before beginning to cook the chilli.
Heat a frying pan – add a little water, fry the chopped onion
garlic and peppers until soft. Add the beef and fry until
browned, add the chilli, cumin, cayenne, tomatoes, tomato
paste , 60ml water and the herbs and then bring to the boil.
Simmer for 25 mins stirring occasionally. Stir in the kidney
beans and cook uncovered for around 5 minutes. Remove from
the heat and stir in the chopped coriander.
Remove the potatoes from the oven and cut in half, top with
the chilli and soured cream – then ENJOY!!

Stoved Chicken

Ingredients:
800g Potatoes sliced (7.5kg £2.00 Farmfoods) = 21p
2 onions thinly sliced (79p 1.5kg Farmfoods) = 10p
1 tsp thyme (49p jar Aldi) = 1p
25g butter (95p 250g Aldi) = 9p
2 bacon rashers (£1.25 250g Aldi) = 50p
½ packet chicken drumsticks & thighs (£2.99 1.25 kg Aldi) =
£1.50
600ml chicken stock with all-purpose seasoning 3p
1 bay leaf (10g 52p Asda) = 2p
Grand Total = £2.46

Method:
Preheat the oven to 150 degrees. Arrange a thick layer of the
potato slices in the bottom of a large casserole dish. Cover
with half the onions. Sprinkle with a little thyme and season
with salt and pepper. Heat the butter in a frying pan and add
the bacon and chicken and stir until browned through. Transfer
the bacon and chicken to the casserole dish – save the fat in the
pan.
Sprinkle the remaining thyme over the chicken and bacon,
cover with the remaining onions and finish with a potato layer.
Pour the stock over the casserole and add the bay leaf. Brush
the potatoes with the remaining fat in the chicken and bacon
pan.
Cover and cook for approx. 2 hours until the chicken is very
tender and cooked through.
Preheat the grill and brown the top then remove the bay leaf
and serve.
ENJOY!!

Slow Cooker Tagliatelle Bolognese

Ingredients:
50g Bacon (250g £1.25 Aldi) = 25p
1 onion (79p 1.5 kg Farmfoods) = 5p
1 garlic clove (39p 4 bulbs Farmfoods) = 1p
1 carrot (1kg 69p Aldi) = 5p
1 celery stick (69p packet Aldi) = 6p
300g beef mince (800g £2.50 Farmfoods) = 93p
70ml red wine (£2.99 Baron St Jean Aldi 750ml) − 27p
2 tbsp tomato puree (35p tube concentrate Aldi) = 5p
1 tin tomatoes (31p Aldi) = 31p
300ml beef stock and All-purpose seasoning = 3p
1 tsp oregano (49p jar Aldi) = 1p
225g tagliatelle (95p all supermarkets 500g) = 48p
Grand Total = £2.50

Method:
Heat a little water in a pan and add the chopped bacon –
stirring frequently. Reduce the heat and add the chopped
onion, garlic, carrot and celery then stir until the veg have
softened.
Increase the heat to medium and add the beef mince and stir
until browned. Add the wine and cook until evaporated , stir in
the puree, tomatoes, stock, oregano and season with salt and
pepper. Bring to the boil and then transfer to the slow cooker.
Cover and cook on low for 8 hours.
Serve with the cooked tagliatelle.

Enjoy!

Gammon with cheddar melt bubble and squeak

Ingredients:
4 Gammon steaks (5kg £15.00 Farmfoods) = £2.00
2 onions (79p 1.5kg Farmfoods) = 10p
225g potatoes peeled, boiled and coarsely mashed (7.5kg £2.00 Farmfoods) = 5p
¼ cabbage (49p Aldi) = 13p
50g grated cheese (450g everyday essentials Aldi £1.99) = 22p

Grand total: £2.50

Method:
Cook the gammon as per instructions on the pack – meanwhile:
Fry the chopped onions in a little oil or water, add the sliced cabbage and mash then season, keep turning until becomes crispy then add the grated cheese- put under a grill to melt through then serve with the cooked gammon.
Enjoy!

Scotch Eggs and Baked Beans

Ingredients:
5 eggs (95p 6 free range Aldi) = 79p
50g plain flour (1.5kg 45p Aldi) = 2p
1 packet Cumberland sausages (specially selected £1.09 Aldi) = £1.09
1 tbsp sage (49p jar Aldi) = 2p
100g Breadcrumbs (800g p Aldi) = 7p
Oil for frying
1 ½ tins baked beans (£1.00 3 tins Farmfoods) = 49p

Grand Total = £2.48

Method:
Boil the eggs for 6 minutes and run under a cold tap until they are completely cold, peel and set aside and dust with a 1 tsp flour.
Mix the sausage meat (removed from the skins) and sage then divide into 4 balls, flatten them out on clingfilm and place an egg on each, then using the clingfilm fold the meat evenly around each egg – keep wrapped in the film and chill for 30 mins.
Place the remaining flour, beaten egg and breadcrumbs on separate plates, roll the eggs in flour then egg then crumbs then egg and again crumbs. Chill for another 30 minutes.
Preheat the oven 200 degrees and heat some oil in a pan until very hot and fry for 2 minutes, transfer to a baking tray and cook for 15mins. Drain well and serve with the beans.
ENJOY!!

Pea and bacon pasta Frittata

Ingredients:

150g Macaroni (50p 500g Asda) = 15p
1 onion (1.5kg 79p Farmfoods) = 5p
100g bacon lardons (89p 150g Aldi) = 59p
150g Frozen peas (99p 1kg Aldi) = 15p
6 eggs (95p 6 Free range Aldi) = 95p
100g Greek style cheese (79p 200g Aldi) = 40p
10g fresh mint (87p 150g Asda) = 8p

Grand Total = £2.37

Method:

Heat the grill. Cook the macaroni as per instructions. While the pasta cooks heat a little oil (or water) in a frying pan and add the chopped onion and bacon over a medium heat until golden.
Drain the pasta when cooked and add to the frying pan spreading evenly. Add the beaten eggs and cook for 2 minutes, dot over the crumbled cheese and sprinkle with chopped mint.
Cook for approx. 10-12 minutes and then put under the grill for 5-5 minutes until browned and set , sprinkle with the rest of the mint then serve and ENJOY!!

Savoury Pasta slices and Roman Baguette

Ingredients:
60g conchiglie pasta (500g 45p Aldi) = 6p
60g Lean cooked ham (£2.99 roasted ham joint Aldi 500g) = 36p
60g mature cheddar (£5.00 1kg Farmfoods) = 30p
½ bunch spring onions (45p bunch Aldi) = 23p
1 tbsp mixed herbs (49p jar Aldi) = 2p
2 eggs beaten (95p for 6 free range Aldi) = 30p
1 French baguette (59p for 2 Aldi) = 30p
1 packet low fat mozzarella (44p Aldi) = 44p
4 tomatoes (49p for 6 Farmfoods) = 32p
1 tbsp lemon juice (39p 250ml Asda) = 2p
1 tsp oregano (49p Aldi) = 1p
50ml olive oil (£2.09 750ml Aldi) = 13p

Grand Total = £2.49

Method:
For the pasta slices:
Preheat the oven to 190 degrees 170 for fan assisted. Grease an 8 inch cake tin. Bring a small amount of water to the coil and add the chopped spring onions cook for 3-4 minutes.
At the same time bring a 2nd saucepan to the boil and add the pasta cook until just about tender. Set aside the pasta and spring onions until cooled. Mix together the onions, pasta, ham, cheese, herbs and eggs seasoning well. Bake for approx. 30mins until set and golden.
This can be served hot or cold.
For the roman baguette:
Soak 4 skewers in water. Cut the bread into 1 inch slices and also the mozzarella (thinly) & tomato (quite thickly).
Combine the oil, lemon juice and oregano in a small dish. Brush generously over the bread slices and then thread the bread, mozzarella and tomato alternately on the skewers. Place on a baking sheet and pour over the remaining oil on the

skewers. Bake for 6 – 8 minutes until the bread is crisp and
cheese is melting. (Turn over carefully halfway)
Serve with the pasta slices and ENJOY!!

Creamy Smoked Mackerel Pasta (Low Fat)

Ingredients:
200g smoked mackerel fillets flaked (£1.59 200g Aldi) = £1.59
200g fusilli (45p 500g Aldi) = 18p
100g half fat crème fraiche (79p 300g Aldi) = 26p
20g fresh parsley (49p 25g Aldi) = 39p

Method:
Boil the pasta until tender, Toss the pasta with the other ingredients and serve in warmed bowls and plenty of black pepper.
Enjoy!!

One Tray Roast Chicken

Ingredients:

510g Chicken quarters (510g £1.15 Aldi) = £1.15
600g new potatoes (59p 1kg Aldi) = 35p
2 tbsp fresh lemon thyme (70p 31g Asda) = 10p
1 garlic cloves (39p 4 bulbs Farmfoods) = 2p
2 leeks (3 for 69p Aldi) = 46p
1 red pepper (3 for 49p Farmfoods) = 16p
100g cherry tomatoes (250g 59p Aldi) = 23p

Grand Total = £2.47

Method:

Preheat the oven 200degrees and 180 fan assisted. Boil the potatoes for 10 mins until just tender. Mix the herbs and garlic and slash the chicken with a sharp knife then rub the herb mixture over the chicken portions.
Drain the potatoes and tip into a large roasting tin, add the chopped leeks and chopped pepper. Arrange the chicken joints over the top and season with black pepper.
Roast for 10 minutes and then stir everything round. Cook for another 10 minutes then add the cherry tomatoes. Cook for another 10 minutes and then check that the chicken is cooked (skewer the thickest part of the chicken and ensure the juice runs clear).
When cooked serve and Enjoy!!

Thai Green Chicken Curry with boiled rice

Ingredients:
400g Chicken Breast (5kg £15.00 Farmfoods) = £1.20
1 tin coconut milk (79p Aldi) = 79p
2 bags rice – boiled (59p 4 bags Aldi) = 30p
2 tsp green Thai paste (59p Home Bargains) = 5p
1 onion (79p 1.5 kg Farmfoods) = 5p
2 garlic cloves (39p 4 bulbs Farmfoods) = 2p
50g stir fry veg (66p 500g Farmfoods) = 6p
½ tsp lazy chili (Home Bargains 59p Jar) = 1p

Grand Total = £2.48

Method:
Chop the chicken into small pieces, and fry with the chopped garlic and Thai paste in a little water. Add the chopped onion and fry till soft, stir in the chili and veg – keep stirring and mixing together. When all is softened and the chicken is cooked add the coconut milk and simmer until bubbling. Serve with the boiled rice and
ENJOY!!

Brie and Tomato quiche with Jacket potatoes

Ingredients:
1 onion (79p 1.5kg FF) = 5p
1 courgette (3 for 89p Aldi) = 30p
2 eggs (95p for 6 free range Aldi) = 30p
150ml milk (£1.80 8 pints Farmfoods) = 6p
60g grated cheddar (450g £1.99 Aldi) = 26p
60g French Brie (200g 99p Aldi) = 30p
1 packet shortcrust pastry (3 for £2.00 Farmfoods) = 66p
½ punnet cherry tomatoes (59p Aldi) = 30p
400g potatoes to make jacket potatoes (7.5kg £2.00 FF) = 10p

Grand total = £2.33

Method:
Preheat the oven 220 degrees, wash and pierce the potatoes
and wrap in foil, bake for approx. 1/2 hour.
Roll out the pastry and line a flan tin (approx. 8 inch) Heat a
little oil in a pan and ass the chopped onion, chopped courgette
and cook until softened – but not browned. Allow to cool.
Whisk together the eggs and milk season well then stir in the
cheddar cheese, onion and courgette. Spoon into the flan tin
and arrange thinly sliced brie and halved cherry tomatoes over
the top. Place the quiche on a PREHEATED baking tray and
cook for 30-35 minutes (leave the potatoes in as well) When
browned and set serve immediately with the jacket potatoes.
ENJOY!!

Low fat Chicken Fricasee and Boiled rice

Ingredients:
1 onion (1.5kg 79p FF) = 5p
2 garlic cloves (39p for 4 bulbs FF) = 2p
350g Chicken Breasts cut into strips (5kg £15.00 FF) = £1.05
150ml chicken stock and all-purpose seasoning = 3p
1 tbsp. plain flour (1.5kg 45p Aldi) = 2p
60ml white wine (£2.99 Baron St Jean Aldi 750ml) = 25p
200g mushrooms (500g 66p FF) = 26p
1 tbsp tarragon (70p 31g Asda) = 10p
2 tsps Dijon mustard (185g 58p Asda) = 3p
150ml skimmed milk (£1.00 4 pints Aldi) = 15p
30g fat free fromage frais (500g £1.00 Asda) = 6p
1 tbsp fresh parsley (49p bag Aldi) = 10p
2 bags boiled rice (59p for 4 Aldi) = 30p

Grand Total = £2.42

Method:
Fry the chopped onion in water until soft and add the garlic
and chicken strips. Season well and cooked for 2-3 mins until
the chicken is sealed.
Sprinkle the flour over the top and cook for a further 1 minute.
Stir in the white wine and stock a little at a time. Add the
mustard, mushrooms, herbs and milk, simmer and stir
continuously until the sauce thickens and the chicken is cooked
through. After around 7 minutes remove from the heat and stir
in the fromage frais. Season and serve with the boiled rice.
Enjoy!

Low Fat Chicken Chasseur with new potatoes

Ingredients:
1 onion chopped (1.5 kg 79p FF) = 5p
400g chicken breasts cut into 4 pieces (5kg £15.00 FF) = £1.20
2 garlic cloves (39p 4 bulbs FF) = 2p
1 tbsp plain flour (1.5kg 45p Aldi) = 2p
3 tbsp dry wine (750ml Baron St Jean £2.99 Aldi) = 25p
1 tin chopped tomatoes (31p Aldi) = 31p
1 tbsp tarragon (70p 31g Asda) = 10p
115g mushrooms (66p 500g FF) = 15p
200ml chicken stock and a/p seasoning = 3p
400g salad potatoes (59p 1 kg Aldi) = 23p
100g peas (1kg 99p Aldi) = 10p

Grand Total = £2.46

Method:
Preheat the oven to 200 degrees.
Fry the onion in a little water, season the chicken on both sides
and then remove from the pan and place in an ovenproof dish.
Add the chopped garlic and add 2 tbsps stock to the pan   stir
in the flour and gradually add the stock, wine and the tomatoes
– stir continuously.
Add the tarragon and mushrooms and bring to the boil – pour
over the chicken and cover with a lid or tin foil. Place in the
oven and cook for 30-35 minutes – until the chicken is cooked
through. Serve with the boiled new potatoes and peas.

Chicken Liver Stroganoff and boiled rice

Ingredients:
450g Chicken livers (227g Asda 50p) = £1.00
1 onion (1.5 kg 79p FF) = 5p
2 garlic cloves (39p 4 bulbs FF) = 2p
1 tbsp plain flour (1.5kg 45p Aldi) = 2p
150ml chicken stock & all-purpose seasoning = 3p
2 tsp Dijon mustard (185g 85p Asda) = 3p
200g mushrooms (66p 500g FF) − 26p
200ml fat free fromage frais (500ml Asda £1.00) = 40p
30ml dry sherry (£5.00 Asda 750ml) = 19p
Pinch paprika (49p jar Aldi) = 1p
2 tbsp parsley (70p 31g Asda) = 10p
2 bags boiled rice (4 bags 59p Aldi) = 30p

Grand Total = £2.41

Method:
Check the defrosted livers for sinew and fat. Rinse and dry on kitchen paper. Preheat a non-stick pan and add the chopped onion and garlic then cook for 3-4 mins.
Toss the liver in flour and season well. Cook quickly over a high heat for 1 minute then add the sherry and gradually the stock − stirring all the time for form a thickened sauce.
Sprinkle the mushrooms over and stir in the mustard, cook for a further 1 minute. The livers should be firm but not overcooked. Remove from the heat and stir in the fromage frais and parsley, season with salt and pepper and serve with the boiled rice.
ENJOY!

Risotto Alla Parmesan

Ingredients:
1 onion (79p for a bag 7 – 8 from Aldi) = 10p
2 cloves of garlic (39p 4 bulbs Farmfoods) = 2p
400g Arborio/Risotto rice (500g £1.10 Asda / Tesco) = 88p
1 3/4 pints veg stock (Maggi stock pots £1.00 for 4 from
supermarkets) = 25p kept simmering...
125g Parmesan (190g £1.30 Tesco) = 81p
40ml white wine (750ml Baron St Jean Aldi £2.99) = 15p
Grand = £2.11
(Garlic baguette 34p Aldi) baked

Total with bread = £2.45

Method:
Melt a little butter in a pan and add the chopped onion / fry
until softened. Add salt and pepper and the wine and boil until
dry.

Add the rice and cook 1-2 mins and add a ladleful of the stock-
on a medium heat stirring until absorbed. Keep adding the
stock a ladleful at a time stirring until absorbed until all the
stock has gone.

Fold in the parmesan and half a teaspoon of butter season with
lots of ground black pepper Then serve on heated plates with
the baguette and ...
ENJOY!!

Slow Cooker Lamb pie with Mustard Thatch

Ingredients:

450g minced lamb (2 x 800g bags for £4.00 Farmfoods) =
£1.75
1 finely chopped onion (79p bag 7-8 Aldi) = 10p
2 celery sticks (49p Aldi for approx. 8 sticks) = 12p
2 carrots (79p 1kg bag Aldi) = 6p
1 tbsp cornflour added to any stock (10for 20p Tesco value) –
5p
800g potatoes (7.5kg Farmfoods £2.00) = 16p
1 tbsp. Worcs sauce = 1p
2 tsp dried ...Rosemary (49p 50g Aldi) – 2p
4 tbsp. Wholegrain mustard (Morrisons 175g 57p) = 2p
4 tbsp. milk and 4 tbsp. milk price depends on what you use
seasoning.

Grand total for 4 = £2.29

Method:

Heat a non-stick frying pan and add the lamb cook until brown
and add the chopped carrots/onions and celery and cook for 2-
3 mins – stirring all the time. Pour in the stock/cornflour bring
to the boil while stirring all the time. Remove from the heat
add Rosemary / Worcestershire sauce and season well.

Transfer to the slow cooker and cook on high for 3 hours or
low for 7 hours.

Towards the end of the cooking time boil the potatoes and
when cooked drain/add mustard milk and butter and make
mash. Spoon that on top of the lamb spread evenly and cook
for a further 45 mins.

Then serve and ENJOY!!!

Minced beef & onion pies

Ingredients:

500g Mince Beef (£2.49 Everyday essentials Aldi 1.5kg) = 83p

1 onion (79p bag of 7-8 Aldi) = 10p

1 tbsp tomato puree (35p tube of concentrate Aldi) = 5p

1 1/2 tbsp plain flour (49p 1.5kg Aldi) = 5p

75g mushrooms (500g 66p Farmfoods) = 8p

250ml beef stock (10 for 20p Tesco Value) = 2p...

Dash of Worcestershire sauce = 1p

Ready-made shortcrust pastry-packet (Heron foods / Cool Traders /Aldi – most supermarkets) 59p

Splash of milk to glaze

400g potatoes to make mash (£2.00 for 7.5 kg bag Farmfoods) = 10p

250g frozen peas (99p 1kg bag Aldi) = 25p

1 serving gravy (Quixo meat gravy 75p for approx. 23 servings – Aldi) = 3p

GRAND TOTAL FOR 4 = £2.11

Method:

Preheat the oven to 200C/400F/Gas 6.

Heat a little oil in a deep frying pan and fry the beef mince for 4-5 minutes, breaking it up as it cooks. Add the onion and cook for 2-3 minutes, then stir in the tomato purée and cook for 2-3 more minutes. Stir in the flour and cook for a further minute, then add the chopped mushrooms, beef stock and a couple of dashes of Worcestershire sauce. Bring to the boil, then reduce the heat, cover the pan with a lid and leave to simmer for 20 minutes. Set aside and leave to cool, then turn the meat mixture into a pie dish.

Roll out the pastry on a floured work surface until it is slightly larger than the pie dish. Gently drape the pastry over the dish, pressing firmly onto the edges. Trim, then crimp the edges with your fingers or a fork. With any leftover pastry cut out some leaf shapes and add them to the top of the pie. Make three or four slits in the pastry to allow the steam to escape, then brush the pie with the milk and bake in the oven for 20-25 minutes, or until golden-brown.

Whilst the Pie is baking boil the potatoes to make into mash or leave as boiled potatoes / also boil the peas approx. 5 mins before the end of the pie cooking time.

Make up the gravy and serve immediately

ENJOY!!

Slow Cooker – Cowboy Pie

Ingredients:
500g Minced beef & onion (800g bag Farmfoods 2 for £5.00)
= £1.56
2 Tablespoons Worcester sauce = max 5p
1 tin baked beans (24 p Aldi) = 24p
1 bay leaf (49p box Aldi) = 1p
200ml beef stick (20p for 10p Tesco Value range) = 2p
750g potatoes (7.5 kg £2.00 – Farmfoods) = 15p
Splash of milk and butter to make mash.
Cheese sprinkle if required.

Grand total for 4 = £2.03

Method:
Preheat the slow cooker. Fry the minced beef and onion with
water or oil if preferred. Add the Worcester sauce and baked
beans, the bay leaf and stock, add salt & pepper then when
gently bubbling spoon into the slow cooker pot and cook for 7-
8 hours.

Top with the mash then if required add cheese and brown
under the grill until browned.

Serve and
ENJOY!!!

Pasta & Pesto with Fresh Basil & Parmesan

Ingredients:
500g spaghetti (23p Aldi 500g) = 23p
50g Pesto (190g 99p Aldi) = 25p
1/4 pot fresh basil leaves (torn) 89p living pot from Aldi = 22p
Parmesan 10g (Tesco£1.30 190g) = 26p
1 Garlic Baguette (34p Aldi) = 34p

GRAND TOTAL FOR 4 = £1.30

Method:
Bake the Baguette as per instructions

Cook the spaghetti until soft – drain the water and add the
pesto until all mixed together. Cover with the parmesan and
basil – then serve with the garlic bread and ...
ENJOY!!!!

Bunny Chow

Ingredients:
1 onion, chopped Aldi 79p bag) = 10p
1 clove garlic, crushed (39p 4 bulbs Farmfoods) = 1p
1/2 tsp turmeric (all supermarkets in region ...for all the
following spices 50p for 48-50g jar) = 1/2p
1/2 tsp garam masala (as above) = 1/2p
1/2 tsp salt
5gstick cinnamon (Tesco East End 99p 100g) = 5 p
1 tsp grated ginger (lazy ginger 49p jar Home Bargains) 1/2p
1/2 tsp ground cumin (as above) = 1/2p
1/2 tsp mixed curry powder (as above) = 1/2p
1 chilli, finely diced (lazy chilli home bargains 49p jar) = 1/2p
250g minced beef (everyday essentials 750g £2.49 Aldi) = 83p
2 tsp tomato purée (35p tube Aldi) = 5p
150 ml beef stock (20p for 10 Tesco Value) = 2p
1x400g tinned butter beans (39p Tesco East End Range) = 39p
Crusty rolls x 4 (Asda do 4 for £1.00) = £1.00

GRAND TOTAL FOR 4 £2.48

Method:
Heat a little oil @ gentle heat, add the onion and cook until
softened. Add the garlic followed by the turmeric, garam
masala, salt, cinnamon, ginger, cumin, curry powder and chilli
and cook for a couple of minutes. Increase the heat and add the
meat, stirring until browned.

Add the tomato puree and then the stock, stir and simmer for a
couple of minutes.
Add the butter beans and cook the dish gently on a low heat for
about thirty minutes. (drain the beans first) When the curry
mixture is ready – hollow out the crusty rolls and put the
scooped out bread to one side – fill the rolls with the curry mix
– dip in the hollowed out bread and
ENJOY!!!!!!!

Low Fat Moroccan spiced rice & Lamb

Ingredients:

300g Minced lamb (£2.50 500g FF) = £1.50
1 onion (79p 1.5kg FF) = 5p
2 garlic cloves (39p 4 bulbs FF) = 2p
1/2 tsp ginger (49p jar Aldi) = 1p
1/2 tsp cinnamon (49p jar Aldi) = 1p
1 tsp paprika (49p Aldi jar) = 1p
1 tin plum tomatoes drained (34p Aldi) = 34p
1 bag boil in the bag rice (59p Aldi) = 15p
400ml Veg stock with A/P seasoning = 3p
1 Courgette (£1.00 for 3 Asda) = 33p
10g Mint sauce (24p smart price Asda 165g) = 1p

Grand total for 4 = £2.46

Method:

Fry lamb mince in a little water for 5 mins, add the chopped onion/garlic/cinnamon and paprika – stir in well. Add chopped courgettes, uncooked rice and stock, bring to the boil then cover and simmer for 20 mins until the rice is cooked. Add drained tomatoes and mint sauce and heat through then serve
ENJOY!